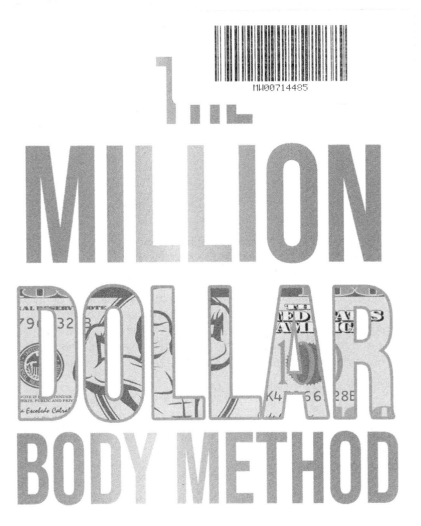

THE MILLION DOLLAR BODY METHOD

The Entrepreneur's Diet for Superhuman Focus and Rapid Fat Loss

NATE PALMER III

Copyright

Printed in the United States of America

First Edition

ISBN: 978-1-7363702-0-9 Paperback

Disclaimer

This book is for reference and informational purposes only and is in no way intended as medical counseling or medical advice.

The information contained herein should not be used to treat, diagnose, or prevent any disease or medical condition without the advice of a competent medical professional.

The activities, physical or otherwise, described herein for informational purposes may be too strenuous or dangerous for some people and the reader should consult a physician before engaging in them. The author shall have neither liability nor responsibility to any person or entity with respect to any loss, damage, or injury caused or alleged to be caused directly or indirectly by the information contained in this book.

If you are taking any medications, you must talk to your physician before starting any nutrition or exercise program, including The Million Dollar Body Method. If you experience any lightheadedness, dizziness, or shortness of breath while exercising, stop the movement, and consult a physician.

Dedication

To my wife Lindsay, for always being on my team.

To all the members of The Million Dollar Body Community for all the help and feedback from you guys. I sincerely appreciate your continued support. Thank you for being a part of my extended family.

Contents

Let me ask you a question: If you could go to the store and buy an apple that INSTANTLY gave you:

10x more energy
10% body fat
10x more focus at work
10x more confidence
10x more motivation to train
A better relationship with your spouse and kids
A healthy relationship with food
Clearer skin
A better immune system
Resistance to injury

What would you pay for that apple? What would you pay for a half of it, or a slice? Maybe the skin that someone peeled off?

If you are like the majority of entrepreneurs, business owners, and high performers out there, the answer is *pretty much anything.*

With these attributes in place, you will have eliminated the chief complaint of 90% of Americans. High body fat percentage and low energy.

Not only do these issues affect our confidence and how we view ourselves, but they create many internal problems for us as well.

For example, visceral fat is a dangerous type of fat that can start surrounding our internal organs after we hit about 15% body fat. It is more damaging than the fat under our skin (subcutaneous fat) because it releases chemicals called *cytokines* that cause full body inflammation.

This can lead to diabetes, heart disease, stroke, and even cancer. The inflammation can cause your brain to be less reactive and less focused, and can create more body fat, more inflammation, and more disease. It becomes a vicious cycle.

Visceral fat also *creates cravings* that make us hungry for sweets and high-carb foods, further compounding these issues by creating more belly fat and ruining the fragile bacterial ecosystem in our gut.

So, we turn to diet and exercise as a means of dropping fat and reclaiming our health.

The single greatest problem for someone who wants to lose weight and get fit is that there are too many coaches and trainers promoting plans and products that are great for helping you drop some weight from your wallet, but not much else.

These "goo-roos" are either intent on increasing their own bottom line in an industry that's set for its biggest year ever (the supplement industry was worth 42 billion dollars in 2019), OR they are coming from a completely unrealistic gym fantasyland where everyone has time to meal prep daily, eat six times per day, and do two-hour workouts before their afternoon nap.

Even well-meaning coaches fall short because a meal plan or rigorous diet does not get to the heart of the issue.

We see ads for programs like

- **7-minute abs**
- **Become the fittest on earth with Crossfit**
- **The Carnivore diet (eat only meat and get healthy)**
- **Veganism**
- **10-day cleanses**
- **7-day water fasts**
- **The Keto Diet**

And so on.

But none of these will be successful long term because of one MASSIVE idea that the entire fitness and health industry fails to mention.

Your weight-loss results DON'T matter

Not even a little.

If it were as simple as losing weight, everyone could be successful. We would all eat grilled tofu and broccoli for two weeks and drop 30 lbs. Starvation diets, cleanses, and other *extreme* measures would be commonplace, and there would no longer be an obesity epidemic in the United States.

This is because, despite the possible good intentions of the people who buy and implement products and diets like this, NONE of them are worth anything if they are not able to be used long term and with good results in your daily life.

So even in the tofu and broccoli example, if you were able to eat that without being bored and disgusted (which is not happening), the first time you eat a bagel, that weight is coming right back to all the wrong places.

What's MUCH more important than hitting your fat-loss goals is being able to maintain your lean, muscular physique, and the rest of your results for life.

95% of people who lose weight through traditional means will gain all their weight back, and more in the next two years.

So, what's the point of putting yourself through months of strain, motivation, willpower, wallet-emptying supplements, and nasty drinks only to have it all come right back?

The fitness goo-roos will often say *"just do an extreme diet for a few months, then you can start eating at maintenance."*

But this is teaching your metabolism to slow down over time.

Not only that, but to keep the results you got from crash dieting, you must Keep. Eating. The. Same. Way. FOREVER.

That is why 99% of coaches and trainers don't talk about this — they don't know how to help people maintain weight loss without huge caloric restrictions and long bouts of cardio that are impossible to keep up over time.

And of course, once you learn this, you are no longer going to be willing to pay for their expertise in showing you how to eat tilapia and broccoli six times per day.

This is why I am writing this book: To help more people understand and connect with the magic of The Million Dollar Body Method.

Simply put, this is a way of eating that is not directly aimed at fat loss, but at something MUCH more important.

The Glycogen Priming Method

The Glycogen Priming Method (GPM) is the key to the Million Dollar Body method. It is a framework that encompasses the nutritional side of the program, and the key to getting great results in your focus and fat loss without hours of meal prep or marathon workouts.

By learning how to use Glycogen Priming in your own life you'll be able to lose fat at will and keep it off easily.

You will be able to summon more energy for important projects, whenever you need it.

You will have the extra capacity to *show up* for your family and friends when it matters.

You will be able to get down to 10% body fat, build an incredible physique, and conquer any physical goal you set for yourself easily.

This is something that the Keto Diet or Whole 30 can never teach you.

Coaches and dieticians have no idea how to get you these results.

And many high-level nutritional experts will not tell you these things because it means they're not going to be able to sell you anything.

So where can you learn how to use Glycogen Priming to accomplish your physical goals easily and use it for a lifetime of success in your physique, your focus, and your finances?

You can learn it from the book you are holding in your hands. A book that is completely different from anything else on the market right now. **The Million Dollar Body Method.**

Obviously if you are reading this right now, you're at least interested.

You probably want to know more, to learn about the "secret" of nutrition that has been withheld from you.

You're probably a bit skeptical, too.

If you're like most people, this sounds too good to be true.

Or like there is a secret pitch coming.

I get it.

There are so many snake oil salesmen in this business that if you jumped in with abandon, I would be concerned about you.

That's why I am going to take some time to tell you about who I am and why you should listen to me.

I'm not out here to take your money in a desperate cash grab before slinking away to my lair in Barbados laughing maniacally as you eat your 23rd meal of pure kale.

I want to tell you why you have never heard of this type of eating before, and how it came to be, as well as some of the stories from others who have used Glycogen Priming to get the results they wanted — not just by losing weight, but by supercharging their focus and energy as well.

Let's get to it.

WHO IS NATE PALMER?

This is the part of the book where I have to establish credibility and make sure you know that I'm not just peddling some supplements that I want you to buy.

We can start with childhood because it's relevant here.

I was a super scrawny kid. Growing up, girls used to make me flex next to them to show that my arms were smaller than theirs.

Kinda funny, right?

Not when you're 12. Then it's the most humiliating shit in the whole world.

One day when I was in 8th grade, I was getting ready for school after my mom had left the house for the day.

There was a knock on the door, and a burly man in a low hat that I did not recognize was out front. As a generally frightened person (heights, strangers, social situations), I did not even open the door.

It was not until he came around back and started peering in the windows that I got a little concerned. And it was not until I heard the back door open that I started to freak out.

I did what anyone would do in my situation. I grabbed a steak knife from the kitchen, and I ran into my bedroom and hid under the bed.

The minutes dragged on as I cowered in fear, ready to stab anything that presented itself in front of my hiding place. Suddenly I heard footsteps coming down the hallway toward my room, followed by him banging on my door.

It might have been a few seconds. It might have been a few minutes. All I know is that I was frozen with fear and incapable of rational thought. Instead of calling the police (because I i getting in trouble), I called my 75-year-old grandpa to come investigate.

The man left with jewelry, cash, and a VCR, and I never saw or heard about him ever again.

Even though this left me with an even deeper fear of the world at large, I also had a burning desire to never feel powerless like that again.

Like many of us, I fell into nutrition and training because I was afraid and running away from something.

Many of us want to avoid the pain of feeling:

- Self-conscious
- Awkward
- Powerless
- Unattractive
- Fat
- Skinny
- Lethargic
- Etc.

And so, we work on changing our bodies in order to escape something.

For years, I labored in the gym trying to get away from the feelings of worthlessness and powerlessness.

But after years and years of training and working to build a meat suit that would "protect" me from the things I was afraid of, I discovered an even more important truth.

The changes don't come from more muscles or revealing your abs. The real change takes place from who you become from the daily, consistent repetition of tasks that improve your body and mind.

I thought I would be happy if I looked a certain way or weighed a specific amount, if I was a mass of veiny muscles, or looked like a comic book hero (or villain...)

But the real transformation came from committing to a task over weeks, months, years, and finally decades. Something that was not always fun, that didn't always feel good, but that got done anyway.

The real reward was the self-confidence that came with keeping the promises I made to myself about showing up daily and running TOWARD improvement rather than AWAY from pain.

I don't say this to brag or to tell you how great I am.

I am average at a lot of things, and bad at most others. But I do have one thing going for me that has made it imperative to write this book. I have spent the past 20 years looking for ways to improve, which has finally culminated in one of the best nutritional frameworks in the world that will spill over into the other areas of your life and help you create radical results in ways you never believed possible.

WHAT IS THIS BOOK ABOUT?

"I feel like I've had a cold for the past 4 years, but I never realized how bad I felt!"

In January 2018, I was doing a routine client check-in with a good buddy who had signed on to my program a few weeks prior.

This was someone I had known in college who had gotten a great job right after graduation. Making close to six figures, he was every bit of what we would consider "successful" in the U.S.

After working for a corporation for a few years, he started his own business and was incredibly successful. Hard work, talent, drive — he had it all. This was a guy who was not afraid of putting in 14-hour days to close new client accounts. Someone who would go 2 hours out of his way to pick up a new contract.

The epitome of hustle.

But something was off.

He had been telling me for a few years that he felt drained. That the spare tire he had accumulated from late-night snacking and weekend beers was not going away, and that literally the last thing he wanted to do after a full day of work was go to the gym, even though he "knew he needed to."

Hell, even the work that had been invigorating for him no longer piqued his interest.

He told me that he felt like he was in low-power mode all the time. Nothing inspired him, and even hanging out with his kids after work required a pep talk or a power nap.

Success was not what he thought it would be.

Let's rewind to 2014, when I wrote an article titled, "How to Eat for All Day Energy" for an online publication. I talked through a nutrition framework I was personally using as a trainer working 10–14-hour days to make sure I showed up for clients with a ton of energy at 6 a.m. and still had what I needed to train my clients at 8 p.m.

It was a bit outside the box compared to normal diets as the focus was not on weight loss but simply maximizing energy and mental focus throughout the day while making sure nutrition aided in improved sleep.

I sent this article out to people 5-10 times per week as I continued to see clients regressing and relapsing from the traditional "eat less, move more" mentality.

So, when my buddy came to me complaining about energy, mood, poor sleep, and lack of focus during the day, I sat down with him to come up with a perfect nutrition plan to help alleviate the issues that had plagued him for years.

He mentioned that fat loss was also a priority, but I talked him out of even thinking about that goal. We did not have any workouts planned, no Tupperware, and not a single piece of kale to be found anywhere.

"If you chase two rabbits, you won't catch either one," I told him, "so let's focus on the most pressing issue. Your energy is garbage, and your wife doesn't want to talk to you because you're always grumpy."

We gradually changed his daily nutrition to reflect his new goals:

- Insane energy on demand
- Mental focus as needed in his business
- Deep, restful sleep
- Waking up every day feeling dialed in
- No more food "hangovers"

Which brings us back to where we started.

"It's like I've been plugged into a socket and finally gotten a full charge. I feel like I've had a cold for the past 4 years, but never realized how bad I felt!"

He raved about how he was feeling, but then came the real mind-blowing piece.

"I also dropped 22 lbs. since I started eating like this, without working out, and without even noticing."

That was the point at which I knew we were onto something special.

This was a guy who had tried multiple diets and had been to every gym within a 5-mile radius but could not stick to a plan.

Everything felt too restrictive and forced him to do things that drained his energy more, while putting his willpower to the test every single day to stick to a "diet."

But a simple framework that allowed him to do the things he loved at a high level? It was a no-brainer! Since his biggest goals were building his business and making more money, structuring his meals to help him do that not only made sense, it made dollars!

THE MILLION DOLLAR BODY PROGRAM

Since that time, I have started working primarily with business owners and entrepreneurs to help them use this same system in their lives to create big changes in energy and drop visceral belly fat easily.

The problem I kept running into was that I could only help a small number of people at a time with this method.

And everyone who successfully implemented this framework in their lives told me the same thing:

"I've literally never even heard of this before."

If my mission is to help as many high performers as possible, that is not feasible behind the closed doors of a program or membership site.

I want to bring this framework to as many people who can benefit from it as possible, even if that means giving away my "secret sauce."

Many of my coaches and friends have advised against doing this, saying that it will eliminate the need to hire me, or reduce the amount of people in my coaching programs.

GOOD.

As a trainer and coach, my goal is always to decrease my clients' reliance on me. If we are still having the same conversations a year into working together, *I HAVEN'T DONE MY JOB.*

So I want to pull back the curtain on one of the most successful nutritional protocols I've ever seen, and give it ALL away, piece by piece, in this book

What Mindset Should I Have with this Program?

One summer between my sophomore and junior year of college, I wanted to make some extra money to "get ahead" for the next year, as well as gain some experience to be able to apply for a job selling ads for the daily paper at the University of Arizona.

I drove my car from Arizona to Nashville for a week-long sales camp, then onward to my destination of Ashtabula County, Ohio.

Six days per week from 8 a.m.-9:30 p.m. I knocked on doors, selling books to families to help their kids with school.

I was terrified of everything at first. Of knocking, of people's dogs, of police, of people saying no, and crazy enough, of people saying YES.

One of my good friends sent me a 60-minute clip from legendary sales trainer Tom Hopkins. He told me it was perfect for what I was doing, and that it was something that would help me get over my fears and start selling more RIGHT away.

I spent 81 hours per week selling books door to door, which included HOURS of commuting time that summer. I literally put 16,000 miles on my car in three months. Want to guess how many times I listened to this sales training?

Zero.

Not a single time.

I always had it nearby, but the truth was that I feared succeeding MORE than I feared failing.

I was scared of what success would mean if I were able to make daily sales, and of what that would mean about my excuses and my previous failures.

It was much easier to have the information but never take action. It was safe. It did not challenge me to do any better.

This book is written as a 28-day program to be followed. The reason it's like that is because too many people are information addicts, but resist doing anything with the info they read.

Information is everywhere, and even radical, impressive information is free online, making it basically worthless.

A program is different from information.
A program requires a start date and an end date. A program anticipates results.
Information is a noun.
A program is a verb.

A program like this will challenge you to take action. Because the only way any of this will make a radical difference in your life is if you make a move on it.

There are **seven** Daily Investments in this program, with **NUTRITION** being front and center.

In order to see results on this program, don't cut corners. Do not amend the program. There is no **My Million Dollar Body Method.** There is only THE Million Dollar Body Method. If you do not do it as described, you didn't do it.

Your mindset around doing this program should be like a scientist, rigorously applying the principles without fail for 28 days so you can decide at the end whether the juice was worth the squeeze.

Or in this case, if going without orange juice in the morning is helping you be more energetic and drop weight easily. Only by fully applying these concepts will you be able to see the complete results you are looking for and decide if this is a viable option for your life going forward.

At the end of the program, you might change the morning routine, you might tweak your midday meal, or you might decide that you have other physical goals, like running a marathon. These are all good things, but the initial 28 days is paramount to your success.

So, follow the directions, check the boxes, and make sure you adhere to this simple framework, every day for 28 days.

I promise, you will not regret it.

What results should I expect to see?

You are going to feel more alert and focused.

The biggest thing reported across the board is a massive increase in energy. Most people who finish the program say they feel "much" more energetic in the morning, but the biggest difference they notice is after lunch — when they normally would start yawning and feel like they needed a nap to refocus. Now, they have more clarity, mental acuity, and are dialed in for their afternoon tasks.

This is one of the most important pieces to the program.

So many entrepreneurs and business owners wear MANY hats daily, so to lose 2-4 hours each day due to fatigue from lack of sleep, the wrong type of food, or poor circulation and breathing, is LITERALLY taking money out of their pockets.

If your competition is falling into a mid-afternoon slump but you have vibrant energy until dinner, who do you think will be first to market or capture more clients?

I don't claim to be able to help you make more money. I don't know how to film a commercial, and I'm pretty bad at Facebook ads, but I *can* tell you that those who complete the program get MORE done in LESS time and are able to check more boxes every day than most of us do in a week.

You are going to lose fat.

Obviously, results differ for everyone. Someone who has been sedentary for 20 years and weighs 350 lbs. might drop 50 lbs. in a month, while someone who is 165 lbs. and active might see their body change and not the scale.

Most people report losing upward of 10 lbs. in 28 days. We have seen as high as 51 lbs., but again, it depends on where you are starting from.

You are going to sleep better.

Most people report falling asleep faster, staying asleep longer, and waking up feeling more rested. I am sure I don't need to extol the benefits of sleeping more, but the CDC recently released a statistic that said getting 5 or fewer hours of sleep per night was equivalent to driving with 2 drinks in your system. [1]

I'm not at my best after a couple margaritas, and you aren't either. So, let's save the libations for Cinco de Mayo and make sure we're using the time in bed to recover physically and mentally so we can crush it while we're awake.

You are going to change your relationship with food.

During this program, you're going to experience food in a way you never have. You're going to learn how to use food as an *input* to determine your experience.

Much like a mathematician manipulating X to get a different result, or a programmer messing with lines of code to change the way something is displayed, you will learn to see food as a "lever" you can manipulate to get the result you want.

And when that result is more energy with an *extremely simple* style of eating, it is a perfect combination for lifelong results.

You are going to improve your blood markers.

A recent study found that out of potential liver transplant donors, 50% were ineligible because they had fatty liver syndrome. [2]

Here is why that's significant.

1. Donors are not sick or obese, so this population is one that already views itself as "healthy."
2. Fatty livers with up to 20% fat ARE accepted, so these people have above 20% of their liver that's *already fat*.
3. 80% of liver donors from cadavers are rejected for being too fatty. (This is more likely the average across the general population.)

Essentially, this means that most of us have an issue with visceral fat, or even worse, organ fat. This causes inflammation, higher cholesterol, high blood pressure, higher fasting glucose, and higher A1C levels.

For those of us without a medical background, A1C is basically a measure of how sticky your blood is from sugar loitering in your blood vessels like teenagers behind the 7-11.

This means more heart disease, cancer, diabetes, and arthritis.

People who complete the 28-day program see remarkable changes in their bloodwork, as well as a decrease in visceral fat — which correlates to being healthier and living longer.

Is 28 days enough to see a difference?

Most people report feeling a difference in their energy and focus within the first week.

People who have reported having a sweet tooth or sugar craving sometimes say that they had a headache for the first 3 days, but that it went away quickly.

This framework has also been shown to fully *reset* your insulin sensitivity in as little as 2 weeks. [3]

One week is usually the amount of time it takes to dial in the process to make it seamless and easy to use in your life, so the majority of the weight loss seems to happen between the 2nd and 4th weeks.

Those results can continue if you follow the program. Most people who are already lean report seeing a difference in the mirror or in progress pictures rather than seeing the number on the scale change. By becoming more efficient at using stored energy (fat) as fuel, the body can burn fat quickly while continuing to build lean muscle.

This increases the rate of the metabolism and obviously is a benefit for anyone who wears a tank top to work.

When first pondering how to disseminate this information, I was honestly not interested in having it built around a four-week program, as it might have the tendency to be looked at as a "cleanse" or "reset," when in reality it was crafted to be a simple lifestyle change.

Most people will either use a derivative of this program long term or return to it if they feel their energy waning, or that they need multiple cups of coffee or energy drink to keep them focused after 2 p.m.

The reason we ended up with a 28-day program is because:

1. Four weeks is a reasonable amount of time to invest in trying something you are unfamiliar with.
2. A set program makes it easier to stay focused, eliminate distractions, and keep away from making random concessions.
3. Having a strong 28-day base gives you a great idea of what the Million Dollar Method will look like in practicality, something that you will not get from a week or two.
4. Enthusiasm for something new or different seems to diminish after week two. Continuing into weeks three and

four will teach you how this method is easy and efficient for everyday life.

Is this just another diet book or morning routine?

> "If diets are so bad and don't give you results, then why write a diet book?"

This is less about a diet and more about a paradigm shift around eating. This book breaks down nutrition in a simple and easy-to-understand way. You don't need to understand the KREBS cycle, autophagy, or pee on a strip 3 times per day to maximize your results.

Because the goal of this framework is first and foremost about creating energy.

That's what makes it different.

Yes, fat loss happens, and that's why people enjoy coming back to this framework as a baseline. But the magic is in how you feel. If you wake up every day feeling like a superhero, why would you ever go back to the lethargy of the Standard American Diet?

Of course, I'll be talking about a morning routine that I believe is integral to the success of the program, but you won't need 3 hours and a special handmade quill from an Argentinian Emu to benefit from it.

Everything in this book is what I believe to be the simplest possible option for optimum results. If you already have a morning routine that includes meditation, journaling, some derivative of the Miracle Morning, or something else you enjoy, you can of course add that into what I already have for you, but if you find that you are low on time, I'd encourage you to stay with the steps outlined in this book.

The goal is not to have this be a personal development book.

Nor is it to be the #1 diet in America — although it would be incredible if everyone in the U.S. started eating this way. It is simply to show high performers and those who live and die on their daily energy that there's a way to automate their focus and mental acuity, daily.

I want this book to enable you to broaden your toolchest of focus and productivity "hacks" to include the breakfast you eat, the way you prepare your lunches, and a dinner that improves your sleep without needing to eat something completely different from your family.

The other reason that this is NOT a diet book is that The Million Dollar Body Method (MDBM) is compatible with other diets you might enjoy.

This method can be done with:

- Paleo
- Whole 30
- If it Fits Your Macros (IIFYM)
- South Beach Diet
- Mediterranean Diet

One caveat is that the Million Dollar Body Method is NOT compatible with:

- Keto
- The Vegan Diet
- The Carnivore Diet

Even though many people label this as "cheater keto" due to the idea of becoming fat adapted and having a higher percentage of calories coming from fat, at no point using the MDBM will you enter ketosis, which also precludes you from the "keto flu" or the headaches that can come from cycling in and out of ketosis.

True keto also calls for a 4:1 ratio of fats to protein which does not serve us here.

Others wonder if a vegan diet can be used on the MDBM, and unfortunately, the answer is no.

It is near impossible to meet the protein requirements with a vegan diet without adding so many carbs that this program would be rendered ineffective.

Veganism is an *advanced* diet that can be used successfully to improve body composition and health markers, but most people without basic knowledge of nutrition will find themselves feeling worse and have a worse body composition from transitioning to a vegan diet.

The Million Dollar Body Method

For the next 28 days, there are seven Daily Investments you need to accomplish each day, aside from one *very specific* day each week which is a secret weapon I'll get into in a minute.

The great news is that you are probably already doing at least 3 of these if you're eating breakfast, lunch, and dinner, so we only need to improve upon what you're already doing.

In business, the only way to success is through identifying the Key Performance Indicators (KPIs) and making sure you accomplish them each day.

If your company has a goal of $10 million in revenue this year, you won't get there by writing "Make 10 mil" on your to-do list and hoping you get to check it off. That's an outcome goal that's almost entirely out of your control.

Similarly, we can't put *"have a ton of energy"* or *"lose 25lbs of fat"* on our to-do lists if we want to have any hope of succeeding.

So, we need to outline and execute on the pieces we control that will give us the outcome we're looking for.

So rather than "make 10 million," we would write "prospect 3 new clients per day," "send daily email offering higher-value packages to current clients," or "No more free beer at employee lunches."

(I don't know what kind of business you have, but when you work for yourself, lunchtime perks can become outrageous.)

Similarly, at the center of the Million Dollar Method are 7 KPIs that we've termed "Daily investments" that need to be done...you guessed it, daily.

These 7 tasks need to be completed every day for 28 days. Did I already write that? Yes. Will I write it again? Also, yes.

I'm 100% inflexible in this because I've seen *over and over again* what happens when people "modify" or "tweak" the program. These are always the result of someone thinking that the program isn't ideal or super convenient.

That's right!

Human beings are the BEST out of any other species at justifying, rationalizing, or compromising to make themselves feel better about shitty decisions they make.

That's why I am such a stickler for this program being done exactly as prescribed. Because if you start by saying, "Well, I'll just switch out my breakfast for my dinner today," then as soon as something else mildly inconvenient arises, it's easy to justify why you "just can't complete the program."

And that's not true.

In fact, this program is designed to be highly convenient, and you WILL be able to make small tweaks to accommodate your specific needs and goals.

But not yet.

Right now, you need to complete the full program, exactly as described, for the full 28 days in order to feel and experience the results that come from a relentless commitment to and mastery of the basics.

Plus, here's the truth.

Conditions will rarely be ideal for you to gain your perfect physique, ideal energy, and the finances you've been striving for.

There will be roadblocks, obstacles, injuries, family emergencies, business trips, client dinners, tailgates, and a million other things I didn't list. You need to be able to navigate and execute when things are not perfect, in order to develop a relentless mentality with your health, otherwise you'll look up in 5 years with the SAME issues and irritations, and you'll have an extra 20 lbs. sitting on your joints.

Don't be the person who runs into an issue after 3 days, 3 weeks, or 3 months and gives up and says they will try again on Monday, in January, or when work settles down.

That's some baby-back bullshit because *life will never settle down.*

Some more truth before we get into the core tenets of this program:

You will get bored.

You might be bored with going on walks. Maybe you will be bored with the same types of food or protein shakes, or perhaps it's a boring workout program. But if you ever want to look in the mirror and think, "I love the way my body looks," you need to become a master of the mundane.

> "I fear not the man who has practiced 10,000 kicks once, but I fear the man who has practiced one kick 10,000 times." - Bruce Lee

Practicing the same kick for the 3,000th time is boring. It probably sucks. I would not know because I'm about as useful in a street fight as a big can of silly string. But the person who can push through the monotony of waking up at the same time daily, doing the same exercises, and having the same breakfast is a threat because they have swapped their need for fancy and exciting in favor of effective and simplistic.

You want fancy and exciting? Buy an insane car and go on amazing beach vacations to show off your new physique.

Don't be the person who needs an "exciting" piece of chocolate cake. That's the mentality that will keep you trapped in a job you don't like, in an unhealthy relationship, and staring at a body you dislike every time you see it in the mirror.

Cutting corners on this program might not seem like the same level as failing to build the business you want, but it's no different.

Demand perfection from yourself, eliminate excuses, accept NO compromises, and you will succeed in every avenue.

With that caveat out of the way, let's dive into the first of the Daily Investments.

HIGH ROI MORNING ROUTINE

Want to know the easiest way to ruin your day? Oversleep.

Miss an alarm and wake up 5 minutes before your first meeting or event, and you're almost guaranteed to have a rough day.

One of my clients told me about a day he was running late after missing his alarm clock.

He was scheduled for an interview with a prestigious marketing firm in his area.

Instead of having time, getting a great breakfast, and being relaxed with plenty of time to prep for his interview, he rushed out the door, coffee in hand, still trying to tie his tie.

Between buckling his seatbelt, turning on the radio, and getting directions, he managed to slosh a bit of coffee on his crisp blue shirt.

Does this sound familiar at all?

He raced to the building, burning through an intersection with an extremely orange light, watching behind him for what he *knew* was going to be police lights, but heaved a sigh of relief when he realized that he had made it without adding a traffic ticket to his list of woes.

As it was, he was already a minute late with a black sedan in front of him pulling into the building at a snail's pace.

It stopped, so he stopped.

It started going again, then a pregnant pause over a speed bump.

As if he were being deliberately held up by some mischievous driver who knew he was running late.

He hit the horn and went around, giving him the, "What are you doing?" hand gesture. Not quite the bird, but enough to let 'em know what's what.

He pulled into a parking space and went upstairs for the interview, where he sat in the waiting room for what seemed like an hour.

In reality, it was closer to 15 minutes, but when you're in a hurry, you know how these things can go.

He finally got the nod to go in for the interview. As he sat down in the plush chairs in the office, the blood drained from my client's face as he realized that the man who was about to do his interview was the very same man he had honked at in the parking lot!

He did not get the job.

The takeaway according to my client: *"Always set two alarm clocks."*

If you lose an hour in the morning, it can take all day to make it up.

The opposite is also true. Waking up with plenty of time to accomplish what you need to before the day gets going is one of the not-so-secret "secrets" of high performers everywhere. It seems like every 22-year-old life coach has their own secret sauce to your morning routine that can vary from 30 minutes of transcendental meditation to walking several miles with your mouth taped shut (*this is real*) and sacrificing freshly harvested quinoa underneath a blood moon (*this is fake*).

But do you need to meditate, journal, pray, have a green smoothie, and write 1,000 words of your autobiography before the sun rises if you want to be productive?

Of course not.

I have tried many morning routines that promise an excellent start to your day. Some are simple, and some are more complicated. I have also tested this with hundreds of clients over a decade of training.

Here's What I Know:

1. High performers are inherently looking for the highest return on investment (ROI) of their time, resources, and energy.
2. A morning routine is imperative to a productive day.
3. A morning routine sets the focus for the day.
4. Complexity kills momentum.

High Performers Need a Great ROI

If your 90-minute morning routine includes some journaling, gratitude, meditation, exercise, and reading for an hour and helps you feel amazing, then that's excellent.

But many of us do not have a ton of time, would prefer more sleep, or have pressing projects that we need to start or finish first thing in the morning when we're at our best (or before anyone else starts needing our time and energy).

So, what can we cut away and still get the amazing start we're looking for?

If you can get a great start to your day and feel the way you want to in 20 minutes versus 90, would you take that trade-off?

For most of us, that's a no-brainer.

That is why I've distilled this down into TWO main objectives for the morning that are guaranteed to give the best ROI on your time and improve your energy and focus without needing a shaman to guide you through a brief morning hallucinogenic trip.

A Morning Routine is Imperative to a Productive Day

Even if you are not doing any of the heavy-duty personal development in the morning, having a routine is still important to set the tone for the day.

Mark Zuckerberg only owns one type of T-shirt.

In addition to displaying a barbaric fashion sense, this is important because it reduces the number of choices he has in the morning. Even though this might seem like a trivial matter, when you wear many hats throughout the day, it's easy to end up with decision fatigue from having to manage hundreds of little decisions daily.

By scripting the first few moves of your morning, you'll be way ahead and have your full energy and focus to bring to bear on important decisions of the day, rather than the difficult choice between two cereals.

Simply waking up at the same time, brushing your teeth, taking a shower, and putting on the clothes you've laid out the night before is a great example of a simple morning routine that sets the stage for a great day.

Alternately, hitting snooze four times, and eating a pop tart while speeding to meet with a client is also an example of a morning routine. You'll be hard pressed to find many entrepreneurs who swear by this method though.

We are going to improve your day by scripting two main objectives that take a very minimal amount of time and pay huge dividends.

A Morning Routine Sets the Tone for the Day

If business is your focus, then having a morning routine framed around doing critical tasks for your business, reading leadership books or listening to marketing podcasts are a great way to shift into that mindset.

If your family is the main priority, listening to a family-oriented podcast or writing a note to your spouse or kids will put you in an excellent state to grow in that way.

If your health and fitness take precedence, then starting with some morning exercise gives you a "health mindset" and begins your day with an investment in your future health. An early decision that snowballs into better decisions for the rest of the day.

But there's a secret benefit many people aren't aware of.

Fitness and exercise are *force multipliers* in every other area of your life as well.

Want to improve your business? Being fit and having more energy will give you more focus and ability to make key decisions. People also work with people they like, and exercise will put you in a better mood.

A new study from the Journal of Labor Research also showed that people who exercise make 9% more money. [4]

Exercise also releases endorphins and improves mood, which is so important as a parent or spouse. The better we feel, the "fuller" we are, and the more energy and enthusiasm we have for those around us. Little things that would bother you normally seem less pressing, and patience is increased.

To be the total package, many people think they need to get their business in line, then work on their families, and figure out so many other variables first, not realizing that fitness and health is a force-multiplier that gives you more focus, energy, patience, ability, enthusiasm, joy, and general feelings of well-being that you can then apply to other aspects of your life.

Fitness is the cornerstone.

That's why the two key objectives for the morning start and end with our health.

Complexity Kills Momentum

One other immutable fact I found was that the more complex a morning routine was, the faster clients were to disengage from it, or worse, NEVER even attempt it to begin with.

And these are not LAZY or BAD people, just as I am sure you're not.

But when things get complicated, our brains often shut down in the face of what I call "*small task syndrome*".

You know the sensation. First, we're opening different apps on our phone, finding a book we ordered last month, a journal, now a pen, and holy hell, what's my iTunes password so I can listen to this podcast?

This is a doomed process.

1 in 10 people will muscle through it and develop competency to where it is no longer complicated, but again, if we can get the same results with less complexity, it's easier to execute on a daily basis.

My filter is always: "Can you explain this to an 8-year-old well enough to have them explain it to someone else without confusion?" If not, you might be bordering on too complex.

That is one of the reasons I'm so adamant that no adjustments or shortcuts be taken on this program. It is already built with simplicity and efficacy in mind, so if you are looking for shortcuts, I can guarantee you won't be successful here.

The First Objective

Wake up and drink 32 ounces of water within 30 minutes of waking up.

That's it. Easy. This is basically 2 glasses of water.
2 regular-sized water bottles.
¼ of a gallon.
1 full shaker cup of water.

Waking up and re-hydrating is extremely important for your daily energy. Most people wake up and pour themselves some coffee before anything else, so even a simple change of adding water first can be a lightbulb moment.

Water in the morning is incredibly important. Here's why:

- It can improve your metabolism and help you digest food more effectively.
- It will keep you from feeling hungry throughout the day, as the body often mistakes thirst for hunger.
- Water lubricates your joints and helps your muscles work better.
- It improves the energy boost you get from caffeine or coffee.
- The more hydrated you are, the more fat you can burn (due to the way fat is removed from the body).
- It fuels your brain.
- Water will "detoxify" your body and use your natural systems to remove waste. No cleanse required.
- Water improves your skin's appearance.
- You will get a jump start on hydrating for the day — decreasing the "catch up" in the evening that can cause you to wake up and pee at night

Like we mentioned before, starting your day like this is a gateway drug to improving other aspects about your health.

But rather than gradually smoking more, buying Bob Marley flags, and eventually waking up to notice that everything you own smells like Patchouli oil, you will gradually start making more health-conscious decisions.

It's a small thing but doing this repeatedly is like investing 50 bucks in a mutual fund each month. Suddenly when you look at your account after forgetting you were even doing it, you'll see a large reward for a small, consistent habit.

The Second Objective

Explosive movement for 60 seconds within 30 minutes of waking up.

This can be jump squats, jump rope, burpees, jumping jacks, plyo pushups, boxing, or jumping on a rebounder trampoline.

The bottom line is that it must be a consecutive 60 seconds, and it has to be explosive.

In this context, explosive simply means using as much force as possible to lift yourself (or an external load) as fast as possible. This generally means jumps and throws, vs the slower moving squats and presses that we normally see in the gym.

NOTE: Please avoid using any incendiary devices as a part of your morning routine.

Can you go longer than 60 seconds? *Of course.*
Can you warm up before doing the explosive moves? *Yes!*
Can you do your workout in the morning and have this be a part of it? *Yes, if it's within the first 30 minutes.*
Can you do yoga? *Instead? No. In addition to? Yes.*
What if my knees are broken? *Do some shadow boxing.*

What if my arms are broken? *Jump up and down on your toes.*
Can I do 30 seconds and then rest and then another 30 seconds? *No.*
But what about all the liquid in my stomach from the water? *Drink a little before and a little after.*

The reason that this is only 60 seconds is that we are going for the MINIMUM effective dose. You will find that this is more potent than your cup of coffee and takes less time to make.

Explosive movements like this also prime our bodies and put us in a specific mental state. That state is called: *Sympathetic Nervous System Dominant.* Also known as "Fight or Flight."

In this case though, I prefer to call it "Shake and Bake" because we're really getting prepared for the day and cueing our body in on the expectation with a specific exercise.

As you can see, these both need to be done within the first 30 minutes of waking up. Other than that, there are no rules on how or when they should be done.

You'll also notice that we're doing one FITNESS piece and one NUTRITION piece, which will help us feel great, move better, and have energy, but also, within 30 minutes of rising, we will have also made two investments in our health and fitness WITHOUT relying on willpower.

The Daily Investment

Drink 32 ounces of water and do 60 seconds of explosive exercise within 30 minutes of waking up.

Up Your Game

Just because those are the minimum daily effective doses and expectations does not mean that you're limited to doing ONLY those pieces. I know many people already have a morning routine that is much more in depth than the one I described.

> "Absorb what is useful, reject what is useless, add what is essentially your own." - Bruce Lee

Here are some ways you can add elements to this morning routine without diluting the structure.

Remember that everything we talk about in this book is aimed at getting a positive return on your energy and investment. So, while meditating for an hour would be great with unlimited time, if you can get similar results in 15 minutes, that's what we will recommend.

Improve Your Hydration

Add Vitamin D drops into your water (or take them at the same time as you drink your 32 ounces).

Vitamin D is more of a hormone than a vitamin, and it can improve your energy, immune system, and bone and teeth density. It also suppresses melatonin production which makes it perfect to take in the morning (and a bad choice before bed).

If you are going to go this route, make sure to get D3 with K2 added. That prevents any leaching of calcium from bones or muscles. Ask your doctor how much you need, but most people should take around 5,000 *ius* per day, especially if you live in a place where you don't get sun most of the year.

Add lemon juice to your water.

Adding half of a lemon can improve digestion throughout the day and can make your water more enjoyable to imbibe.

Improve Your Movement

Explosive exercise has many benefits, as mentioned before. But one way you can make a big difference in how you feel after your 60 seconds of explosive exercise is by approaching it with a "quality over quantity" mindset.

Be more explosive.

Yes, by doing 60 seconds of jump squats, you will feel engaged, motivated, and probably a little out of breath.

But if you focus on being *extremely* explosive — jumping as high as you can and landing quietly in a safe position — you'll increase the effects, energy, and your athleticism as well.

Explosive movements communicate to your body that you need more muscle and less fat to be able to execute and escape from predators. Your body does not know that you're not jumping into a tree to get away from a cheetah.

Use this natural ability that your body already must improve your energy and physique in just 60 seconds per day.

Use explosive exercise to warm up for your training session.

In the past 16 years or so, I have only missed a handful of training sessions. This is not to tell you how awesome Nate Palmer is, only that I have been pretty rigid about scheduling and prioritizing this (much to the chagrin of most of the people who go on vacation with me).

But there was a season where I really struggled getting workouts in.

I was incredibly busy, starting a new job and balancing it with an existing side business I ran online.

It seemed that around 8 a.m., my day would hit fifth gear, and suddenly I would look up to see it was 3 p.m. and I'd still have 4 hours of work left.

It became obvious that if the workout was not done before 8, it either wasn't happening, or it morphed into, "I'll do pushups while I'm making dinner," which is perhaps the least satisfying workout of all time.

Many of us have no choice but to get a training session in during the early-morning hours, and sometimes that takes place within 30 minutes of waking up.

We will talk more specifically about training in Daily Investment 7 but if you're relegated to only training in the morning, you can use this AM routine as a great way to wake up and prepare your body faster.

If you live in a cold part of the world or basically roll out of bed and into the gym, then it is very important to do a 5-minute warm up with some sort of steady-state cardio. Rowing, biking, jogging, jump rope, etc.

10 minutes would be great, but like we stressed before, the best ROI is our major focus for this program.

The best time to start doing a *specific* warm-up for the training you are about to jump into is after finishing the general warm-up to get your blood moving. Here's how to use explosive movements to get prepped faster and train harder.

If it's chest day and you're about to do bench press for your first exercise, start by grabbing an empty bar or some light dumbbells.

Do a few reps, concentrating on great form and moving the weight smoothly.

Now hop up and jump right into your explosive plyometric moves. For a bench press, a great option would be:

- Bench Plyo Pushups — hands on the bench, feet on the floor, push yourself off the bench and catch yourself lightly
- Med Ball Chest Passes — bent over at the waist, doing a chest pass at the ground with a soft med ball, and then catch it on the bounce

These specific moves will help the muscles you're working to activate and allow your central nervous system (CNS) to "release the brakes" on your strength.

From there, continue to build up to your working weights, and if you need a slight boost, add in 3-5 reps of the specific plyometric between sets.

Here are a few examples of the best explosive moves depending on what muscle group you're working:

Chest

- Bench Plyo Pushups
- Med Ball Chest Passes (floor or wall)
- Explosive Band Chest Press
- Hitting a punching bag or pads

Back

- Ski Erg
- Band Straight-Arm Pulldowns
- Rotational Med Ball Throw at wall

Legs

- Squat Jump
- Box Jump
- Jump Rope
- Depth Jump (warm up well before this one)

Shoulders

- Med Ball Overhead Throw
- Band Thrusters
- Band Shoulder Press

Note: the goal is always to use the most explosive movement you can when *accelerating*, and to always *decelerate* under control.

Tune Up

Work on your body in the morning with some foam rolling, stretching, yoga, infrared sauna, or any other self-care of your choice.

If you're nursing a nagging injury or simply want to move better, this is a great way to set the focus on improving your physical health and doing this early can have you walking with a spring in your step for the remainder of the day.

Become Unstoppable

In this morning routine, there is no mention of meditation, journaling, gratitude, reading, listening to something positive, or any of the other mental and spiritual aspects that are included in so many other routines.

This is simply because we will be using a fitness component as a "catch all" to provide us with the maximum result in fewer than 5 minutes.

That does not mean you can't include any of the above practices, or that you need to stop doing what currently works for you.

Here are two other practices that can amplify your morning and help you create the consistency needed to thrive in the Million Dollar Body Method.

WTFU

Don't hit snooze on your alarm clock. Put it across the room if you must. Think about the difference in mentality if your first thought of the day is, "*I'll try again later*" versus making a strong decision to get out of bed on the first ring.

This is how winners think.

Take a cold shower.

This is a prime example of taking decisive action first thing in the AM. Get into a cold shower straightaway or after you work out. Especially when it is chilly out, this can go against everything inside of us, which is *exactly* why we need to do it.

The more reps we get in at telling our inner bitch voice that it does not run the show, the better our life will be.

Not only that, but cold showers wake you up, invigorate you, can help burn fat, improve mental cognition, and make you harder to kill.

Sample Schedule

Here is an easy way to fit these concepts in while maintaining the integrity of the Daily Investments.

These are suggestions and additions. As long as you're:

- Starting the day with 32 ounces of water and 60 seconds of explosive exercise

You'll be blown away by how much focus you have and how fast fat disappears.

6:00 a.m.: Wake up
6:10 a.m.: Drink 32 oz. water
6:25 a.m.: 60 seconds of explosive exercise
6:26-7:15 a.m.: Strength training
7:15-7:20 a.m.: Deep breathing and cooldown
7:20-7:30 a.m.: Cold shower and getting ready for the day

THE ENTREPRENEUR BREAKFAST

I f you've ever walked down the breakfast aisle in your friendly neighborhood supermarket (and I'm sure you have), you'll notice that 99% of the items there will completely ruin your chance at a high-energy day with great focus.

This is because everything we view as a breakfast food in the U.S. is a high-sugar, high-carbohydrate, high-energy source of fuel for our bodies.

Carbs aren't inherently evil but starting your day with an absolute gut bomb of refined sugars and colors that have never been seen in nature is a sure way to start off the day on the wrong foot.

Therefore, Daily Investment 2 focuses on intake of the correct nutrients, vitamins, minerals, and macros during our morning.

If we want to be at our best and feel amazing all day, we need the proper fuel to start the day.

After working with entrepreneurs and business owners for more than a decade, I found that one of the single greatest contributors to low energy, poor performance, and general feelings of malaise comes from our daily breakfast.

Most people DON'T take the time to properly fuel up in the morning.

They think that having a few extra seconds to do work, submit a contract or get dialed in on some aspect of their business will make them more money in the long term.

This is a short-sighted perspective of what's important, especially when you think about how often this happens over the course of a month, year, or a decade.

If they do take the time to eat breakfast, most will make suboptimal selections. Choosing the wrong foods in the morning is a huge reason most people in the U.S. deal with a disease called insulin resistance, or *metabolic syndrome*.

This means that our blood chemicals are no longer functioning properly to allow us to use carbohydrates effectively. Instead of using carbs for energy, we primarily store these as fat, and the resulting chemical reactions in our body cause a slow-down effect that saps energy all day.

How do you know if you have insulin resistance?

- Waist-to-height ratio is greater than 0.46
- Size 42 or larger pant
- Energy and mood swings throughout the day
- Hunger even after a meal

- Blood A1C level above 5.7 (this gets checked in standard blood work)
- Belly protrudes or hangs over pants and belt
- If your fasting blood sugar levels are greater than 126 mg/dL (can check this using a glucometer)
- All Day Fatigue
- Patches of dark skin (*acanthosis nigricans*)
- Acne
- Polycystic ovarian syndrome (*PCOS*)
- Fatty liver disease
- Sugar and carb cravings all day
- Feeling "hangry"
- Scalp hair loss in women
- Skin tags
- High blood pressure
- Fluid retention, swelling in ankles
- High blood pressure
- Trouble concentrating

Insulin resistance is one of the chief reasons that successful, intelligent, proficient people feel sluggish all day and need a nap around two o'clock.

If affected by the disease of insulin resistance, then eating a banana, bagel, or bowl of cereal in the morning will cause your blood sugar to rise.

This is supposed to happen. It's normal.

Think of blood sugar like hotel guests at a swanky, brand-new high rise.

Insulin is like the hotel concierge. As the guests come in, each one is assigned to an employee who makes sure the guests get to the right room and are wonderfully comfortable.

In a healthy body, each guest gets their own concierge and is escorted to the right place in a timely manner.

When our bodies are not balanced, this creates a discrepancy between guests and attendants, so we will either have a ton of pissed-off guests in the lobby, probably writing Yelp reviews about the crummy service, or we have too many employees with nothing to do, walking around and creating havoc.

Neither are good options.

With too much insulin in your system (too many employees), your body starts sending signals that more blood sugar (guests) are required to keep the system working properly, EVEN when the hotel is at capacity.

That's where hunger pangs come from.

Worse, every time you snack to sate the cravings, energy is pulled away from your body and brain to aid in digestion, further reducing your focus and ability to concentrate.

By the time you finish your day, you are exhausted without much physical exertion outside of the work you're doing.

This is a massive problem for many people across the U.S., but thankfully, it is also extremely easy to counteract.

Here's What I Know:

1. The best breakfast for energy consists of high-quality *Proteins* and *Fats*
2. Limit carbohydrates in the morning for better focus
3. Eat LESS for MORE energy
4. Eating the same thing for breakfast daily will make it easy to see results.

The Best Breakfast Consists of High-Quality Proteins and Fats

Protein is an essential nutrient that is important for rebuilding muscle, improving recovery, and giving your body the ability to manufacture the enzymes it needs to stay healthy and create the chemical reactions that build energy instead of stealing it.

Improving upon this by adding some high-quality, healthy fats to your breakfast is a recipe for vibrant energy and intense mental acuity all day.

Proteins and fats are slower digesting than most carbohydrates. This means they cause less of a blood-sugar spike and less need for your body to produce and manage insulin - ideal for someone with even low degrees of insulin resistance.

Healthy fats are also optimal for helping keep your endocrine (hormone) system running well, which can improve mood, energy, and digestion, while staving off many health issues men and women face as we age.

Fat in the morning can also improve upon the energy-enhancing abilities of caffeine. Eating more fat will help the caffeine create more of a mellow, focused, long-lasting "buzz" by slowing down the absorption and giving you a "time release" that will keep your focus on point all day.

To maximize the way your body looks and the way your mind performs, protein and fat for breakfast is an optimal strategy every day

Limit Carbohydrates in the Morning for Better Focus

Even if you do not suffer from insulin resistance, if your body fat is less than 10% or you are trying to gain muscle rather than lose fat, an optimal breakfast to *create extreme amounts of energy* does not need carbohydrates.

In fact, carbohydrates cause your body to slow down to digest them as well as the aforementioned insulin spike that can often keep you from fully feeling satiated and can cause hunger pangs that sap your energy all day.

This is not to say that you can never eat waffles, bagels, or a banana in the morning ever again, but on days you're aiming for optimum performance and mental focus throughout the day, limiting morning carbs will improve your output.

So while we won't be having pancakes during this program, you now know the reality behind those choices and can adapt accordingly.

By the way, the leaner you get, the easier it becomes for your body to handle carbs and sugars, so if you want to be able to eat Saturday morning breakfast foods, focus on dropping body fat first.

Eat LESS for MORE Energy

Thanksgiving is a great time of year where we spend time being grateful for the blessings in our lives, get to see friends and family, and enjoy the feeling of passing out at 5 p.m. after ingesting enough calories to kill a smaller mammal.

Many people blame this on tryptophan, an amino acid found in turkey. Which could be true if you're eating more than a pound of the bird, but for most of us, the post-Thanksgiving fugue state is brought on by stuffing, bread, mashed potatoes, and other high energy foods.

Plus, pork has more tryptophan than turkey, and most of us are not passing out after a ham sandwich.

Big meals put us into "parasympathetic nervous system dominance" (rest and digest), which is a great time to chill out, take some time to unwind and start gearing down to go to sleep.

Overeating can obviously slow you down. But did you know that undereating can have the opposite positive effect of keeping you more energized?

Slight hunger sensations can improve upon your sympathetic nervous system state and allow you to access more energy, have more focus and be more dialed-in to your surroundings or tasks.

As we came from a society of hunters and gatherers, the most ideal time to hunt was NOT after a big feast, but when we were hungry.

Although we no longer need to hunt our food, everyday business owners, real estate agents and commission based salespeople are going out hunting for new leads, prospects, and ways of gaining income for themselves and their family.

Having the mental ability to be dialed in, to be looking for opportunities and to be extremely aware of our surroundings is a huge boon to ourselves, our mentality, and our business. And we can access this superpower extremely easily just by eating light.

For focused work that requires more than an hour of concentration, having low-grade feelings of hunger can aid in next-level focus and getting lost in "flow state."

For these reasons, I strongly advise against feeling full for the first 10 to 12 hours of the day. This alone can improve energy, decrease insulin resistance, and cause your body to burn more fat for fuel, giving you a physical and mental edge over your competitors.

Eat Boring, Win Big

> "Be boring and orderly in your life, so that you may be violent and original in your work" - Gustave Flaubert

Chris Suave of Shopify has a TEDx talk called "The Habits of Highly Boring People". He shares how he and various other rich and famous people take a structured approach to simple thing in their lives to free up energy to focus on the things you enjoy doing.

One of the salient points he makes is about the Paradox of Choice, the title of a book by Barry Schwartz. This basically means that in our day to day lives we have so many options in what to eat, where to go, and even what to wear that our brains basically shut down.

Having to sift through so many options takes mental energy away from the important decisions we need to make daily.

As discussed in the previous chapter about your morning routine, having to choose what you eat for breakfast is a waste of energy.

Will it be a bagel?

Maybe pancakes or French toast because it's the weekend?

Actually, should it be oatmeal because that's heart healthy?

Or maybe there's only granola left, but no milk, drat.

Or maybe you can grab a banana on the way out the door...

Small, simple decisions like this sap you with no payoff, and even if it doesn't seem like a big deal, this can lead to decision fatigue in the later parts of your day.

Don't fall prey to the marketing lie that has been ingrained since Saturday morning cartoons that we need to eat something new and special every single meal of every single day for the rest of our lives.

Instead, find two meals you can easily alternate, and eat them on a regular basis.

This is going to enable you to see what effect your first meal has on your energy and then refine from there.

That way, if you add a supplement or something that claims to give you more energy, you will be able to discern if it's giving you a return on your investment.

When bulletproof coffee gained popularity a few years back, many people started to include it in their mornings and reported feeling a lot more energy!

But since their baseline was a bagel and a latte with 50 grams of caramel, anything would have been an improvement.

That is why in this Daily Investment, we are going to use only one breakfast we can maintain for the entire program, while we focus on the other aspects of our day that give us a great ROI.

Mastery of the mundane is the beginning of results.

The Objective

Make sure your first meal consists of protein and fat, while limiting carbohydrates to less than 15g.

There are dozens of ways to accomplish this, but we are going to focus on the one with the biggest ROI.

We will also be eating the same thing over the course of the program. After the program is complete, it's a good time to branch out and choose another go-to meal that can be cooked and eaten quickly and easily.

Protein and Fat is the best breakfast you can eat. Here's why:

- Protein is highly satiating, meaning it will keep you full longer.
- Protein will help your body and muscles recover.
- Protein breaks down into amino acids, which are used by your body to create *enzymes*, that help your body carry out important chemical reactions.
- Protein and fat are slow digesting, which means they cause a lower blood sugar response.
- Low blood sugar response means less chance to spike your insulin, which will decrease cravings during the day.
- Slower digesting means you will be full longer.
- Fats are great for "low-impact" work. They help us when we're reading, thinking, processing, writing, or doing work that requires concentration without physical exertion.

- Fats can help your body utilize caffeine more effectively and give you a steady drip of consistent energy rather than making you twitchy.
- Most "breakfast" foods are high in carbohydrates that will *decrease* energy throughout the day when consumed in the morning.
- Eating fat can condition your body to use fat for energy

There are other benefits ranging from insulin production to fat burning that make this the right choice for the entrepreneur of the future. As we have said before, this is not the right program for those doing hard physical labor 15+ hours per week, training for an ironman, or building as much muscle as possible.

This framework is specific to those who need more energy and focus to improve their business and finances while still having energy in the evening for their families and those who are important to them.

Awareness is a powerful thing.

Awareness is like reading the lyrics to a song you've known forever and noticing you have some of the words wrong. The next 28 days will be like that. Once you know what your baseline is and how your body responds to certain foods, it's hard to go back to being confused about what to eat.

The Daily Investment

Make a protein shake for your first meal of the day.

- 2 scoops whey protein isolate
- 2 tbsp. natural almond/peanut butter
- 8 oz. almond milk
    - Total carbs at breakfast < 15g
    - Add ice to increase satiety or make thicker

> o Add water to increase volume or thin

Up Your Game

Having a shake in the morning is awesome. It's fast, easy, and doesn't require any prep work. It can also be amended to fit any goals or lifestyle.

You can make a single shake into a huge portion and save some for later, or you can condense it down into a few sips.

It is extremely easy to customize depending on your goals.

Look through the list below and see if there are any other additives you want to incorporate into your shake in the morning. I recommend following the base shake formula to start, as it will give you a good starting point, then it is easier to see if small changes have any effect.

As you experiment and add more "boosts" to your breakfast, you will have a better gauge for what the boosts are doing for you and if they are giving you a good ROI.

These are the main boosts I find helpful, but this is obviously not an exhaustive list:

Caffeine - Boosts energy

Cinnamon - Lowers blood sugar

Sage - Improves memory

Turmeric - Powerful anti-inflammatory

Cayenne - Cancer-fighting, anti-inflammatory

Ginger - Decreases stiffness, nausea.

Salt - Improves cellular hydration

Creatine - Improves ATP/strength

MCT oil (*Fat, can be subbed for almond/peanut Butter*) - Improves caffeine uptake, increases fat burning

Cocoa powder - Improves cognition, increases insulin sensitivity

Maca root - Boosts energy and stamina

Refrigerated banana peel - Resistant starch, improves gut health.

Vitamin C - Cancer-fighting, Immune booster, improves arterial elasticity.

Vitamin D - Improves immune system, increases energy.

Coconut oil (*Fat, can be subbed for almond/peanut Butter*) - Anti-bacterial/fungal/microbial

Lemon - Improves digestion

Reishi mushroom - Fights fatigue, Immune booster

Lion's mane mushroom - Improves mental performance

Leafy greens (*spinach, kale*) - High in phytonutrients

Spirulina - Antioxidant booster, lowers blood pressure

Aloe vera - Antioxidant, immune booster, aids digestion

Avocado (*Fat, can be subbed for almond/peanut butter*) - Anti-inflammatory Omega-3 fatty acid

Bee pollen (*Carb*) - High in phytonutrients, complete protein source

Cacao nibs (*Fat*) - High in antioxidants, minerals

Chia seeds (*Fat*) - High fiber, protein, Omega-3s

Flax seeds (*Fat*) - Boost testosterone, high Omega-3s, fiber

Hemp seeds/hearts (*Fat/Protein*) - High protein, Omega-3s

Nutritional yeast - High protein, mineral, Vitamin B
Walnuts *(Fat)* - High Omega-3s, Vitamin B

Wheat grass - High in antioxidants, phytonutrients, anti-inflammatory
Matcha - High in antioxidants, caffeine

Sample Schedule

Here's an easy way to fit these concepts in while maintaining the integrity of the Daily Investments.

These are suggestions and additions. As long as you're:

- Starting the day with 32 ounces of water and 60 seconds of explosive exercise
- Having a nutrient dense protein shake for your first meal

You'll be blown away by how much focus you have and how fast fat disappears.

6:00 a.m.: Wake up
6:10 a.m.: Drink 32 oz. water
6:25 a.m.: 60 seconds of explosive exercise
6:26-7:15 a.m.: Strength training
7:15-7:20 a.m.: deep breathing and cool-down
7:20-7:30 a.m.: Cold shower and getting ready for the day
7:35 a.m.: Make and drink your protein shake

DAILY INVESTMENT 3:

THE START-UP LUNCH

Here are some crazy statistics:

The energy drink industry was valued at $56 billion in 2018 and is expected to grow to more than $83 billion by 2026.

Most energy drinks contain between 80-400mg of caffeine per

This is creeping up on the coffee industry, which showed revenue of just over $80 Billion in 2019.

The average coffee contains about 80mg of caffeine for a 12-ounce cup of black, drip coffee. Cold-brew coffee and concentrate can contain more than 3 times that amount.

Despite continued education about health, nutrition, and sugar, the soda industry grew by $2.5 billion in 2019 to reach its highest revenue ever, valued at more than $156 billion.

Soda contains about 35-60mg of caffeine per 12 ounces.

For reference, the Mayo clinic says that 400mg is the top end of what an average healthy adult should have daily. [5]

The bottom line here is that we love caffeine and all things energy. Whether sipping a homemade dark roast in the morning per your daily ritual, grabbing an energy drink after lunch to have the focus you need for the afternoon, or relaxing with a coffee after dinner, we consume more energy products than any other country.

Our desire for caffeine is so insatiable that while my wife and I were traveling through Colombia (the number one coffee exporter to the U.S.), it was next to impossible to find a good cup of coffee. Since everything gets exported, locals drink Maxwell House Instant Coffee, which is considered the "good stuff."

When I first started my fitness career, I worked as a trainer at a big gym in Phoenix. We routinely did wild things in the pursuit of getting jacked.

One time that stands out was when my good buddy Mason and I took a red-line energy drink (350mg of caffeine) and added a scoop of N.O.-Xplode to it (250 mg of caffeine) for a regular 4 p.m. workout.

It was a transformational experience because not only was I short of breath just walking to the weights due to my excessive heart rate, but I also had the inability to decrease the volume of my voice, or general grunting. Not great.

But what if you did not need energy drinks in the afternoon for the motivation to hit a workout, finish a project, or to get through the last few pieces of work before heading home to see your family?

What if you could do more work in less time by challenging the traditional concept of lunch?

What damage could you do with an extra hour of focus in the afternoon?

What would that do for your business? Your finances? Your family?

In this chapter, we are going to dive into the optimal lunch if you want to stay highly productive in the afternoon and be able to do more in less time.

We are going to rehash some of the concepts from the previous chapters because they are extremely applicable here as well, and I will continue drilling into them.

So, pay attention, because this is a concept that bears repeating. The more I say it, the better you will be able to understand it fully and utilize these tools in your life to improve your focus whenever necessary.

Here's What I Know:

1. Normal lunches crush productivity, and we are not "normal."
2. You owe your family and clients your best.
3. The right lunch has MACRO and MICROnutrients.
4. Plan, don't prep.

Normal Lunches Crush Productivity, and We are Not 'Normal'

Think about the average American lunch. For the most part, we are talking about burgers, fries, a Chipotle burrito with extra rice, or something deep-fried.

Lunch foods are high-calorie, high-carbohydrate, and high-fat.

The definition of "rich."

That means we need extra time and energy for our bodies to digest that food.

These foods slow us down and use energy for digestion that could have gone to productivity and focus for our businesses or families.

The digestion of these high-calorie, high-carbohydrate lunches are going to pull blood and energy from your appendages and brain and bring it to your gut so that you are better able to break down this food.

This is a healthy digestive function.

However, we want to make sure we are timing our food digestion in a way that serves us best. And breaking down a burger and fries at noon is going to decrease our productivity, and focus, for the remainder of the day because it takes one to three hours to digest a large meal.

If your job consists of you not getting caught reading fantasy football updates, or if you do not have any plans to be productive for the remainder of the day, by all means indulge in that extra-large burrito and spend the rest of the day browsing social media.

But if you are not normal, if you're looking for something more, if you're building something special, or if you need focus to get through the last bit of paperwork before you can go home and see your family, having the "normal" type of meal is going to yield you normal results.

And we are not normal.

You Owe Your Family and Clients Your Best

I recently watched an interview with Kevin Hart, where he talked about the reason why he works out every single day. He knows that training daily keeps him at his best, and if fans come to see him, he owes them the best show possible.

If he were to show up with anything but his absolute best performance, he would be letting down his fans.

How much truer is this for our family?

If you paid a few hundred dollars to take your significant other to see Justin Timberlake, but instead of the high-energy show you were expecting, he moped around, sang a little, took long breaks, and generally gave a half-assed effort, what would you think?

What would your perception of him be?

Most of us would get on our phones midshow to tweet about what a disappointing experience we had from an entitled performer who does not care about his fans.

That is the same for us with the people that we need to show up for daily. If we are not constantly bringing our best for our customers and families, it's easy to think that we don't care.

And that sucks to hear, but there is an easy way to remedy this and to make sure you're showing up for your family in the evening with the same energy as you have for a sales presentation in the morning.

It can be as simple as changing your lunch a little bit to ensure that your energy and focus are on point for the remainder of the day.

Simply by delaying our gratification and eating the right foods, we can be 100% present for the people we love, as well as those who are paying for our time and expertise.

It's a no-brainer, especially if all we're doing is changing how we approach lunch. The most boring meal of the day.

The Right Lunch has MACRO and MICROnutrients

The middle of the day is when we are most likely to get trapped by fatigue or low energy. An easy way to combat this is by eating foods that build energy rather than take it away.

Eating the wrong foods will put us into the exact opposite state and leave us wanting a nap after lunch. With the right MACROnutrients and, more specifically, the right MICROnutrients, we can inject a burst of energy into our afternoon without having to slam a Red Bull or a Monster energy drink.

Luckily, we do not need a master's degree in biochemistry to figure out what the right MICROnutrients are. The simplest way to get the right foods is by "eating the rainbow" of vegetables for lunch.

The easiest and best vegetables to include in your lunch:

- Carrots
- Bell peppers
- Celery
- Cherry tomatoes
- Cucumbers
- Snap peas

Carrots are easy to pack, easy to bring with you, and extremely high in micronutrients, especially the ones that give you energy: Vitamin C, Vitamin A, and beta carotene, as well as specific *"fatty alcohols"* that can assist in burning belly fat. Carrots are the clear winner here.

Other great options are green, red, and yellow bell peppers. Along with celery, these are all high in water content and easy to pack.

Cherry tomatoes, cucumbers, and snap peas are all vibrant colors and easy to take on the go, making them a great choice for a Glycogen Priming Lunch.

The other MACROnutrient we want to make sure we are getting in is protein. As we have talked about before, protein is a source of amino acids to help our body produce the enzymes it needs and build muscle.

Protein is also slower digesting, which is going to give you long-term energy throughout the day. It keeps your blood sugar from spiking, prevents a large insulin response, and can eliminate food cravings.

So, you get the benefit of no crash and no cravings after lunch, simply by changing what you choose to eat.

Eating a light lunch of protein and vegetables like this is also important to avoid getting full. If we stay away from the sensation of being "stuffed," we will have more available energy to work with in the afternoon because we haven't shifted into "rest and digest" mode.

Other easy options to get MICROnutrients here are adding a "green" or "reds" drink to your afternoon to get the vitamins and minerals you need to feel your best all day long.

A greens or reds drink is a powdered supplement made from a variety of fruits and veggies like spirulina, spinach, wheatgrass, beets, pomegranate, and other nutrient dense foods. You can find a ton of good options online, or check out my supplement guide to get my recommendations at n8trainingsystems.com/supplements

That also doubles as a nutritional insurance policy, and a sure way to keep your immune system healthy while getting the nutrients you need.

Plan, Don't Prep

The entrepreneurs and business owners I work with rarely have time to prep new and exciting lunches. Instead, it's best to plan out your food ahead of time and give yourself the option to either grab the right food on the go at a restaurant, or simply pack some carrots and bell pepper strips with two chicken thighs.

This strategy makes it quite easy to eat a healthy lunch.

The best way to accomplish this is by batch-prepping a dozen chicken thighs (or any other protein) on the weekends, and then using kitchen shears to cut up the chicken thigh into a bag or Tupperware that is always easily accessible. Grab a bag of baby carrots, and you're out the door in under a minute.

If you're cooking the dinners described in the next Daily Investment, double the recipe to ensure you always have leftovers. This gives you the ability to quickly reach into the fridge and grab what you need without a complicated or lengthy meal prep.

If you always have some protein batch-prepped and three or four bags of baby carrots in your fridge, at your office, or anywhere else you're going to be, you will always have what you need for the perfect lunch.

Of course, any vegetable will do, but carrots are hardy, filling, and packed with the nutrients you need. There is a secret benefit as well.

A study took two groups of college-aged men and gave one group plenty of beta carotene (which carrots are packed full of) and the other group a placebo. After 12 weeks, females were 50% more likely to rate a male from the beta carotene group as being MORE attractive than they were prior to the study. [6]

Baby carrots will change your life.

The Objective

Eat proteins and veggies for lunch.

Protein and veggies are the optimal lunch, ESPECIALLY if you want to get more done in the evening than ever before. There are basically unlimited ways to combine those into a great lunch, but for now, we want to keep it simple and avoid complications.

Try to pick two options to alternate between daily if you tend to have the same lunch schedule. If you have variable days, i.e., you drive all day Tuesdays and Thursdays but in the office at all other times, pick one driving lunch and one office lunch.

Complexity kills momentum. Keep it simple.

Protein and veggies for lunch is the best lunch you can eat. Here's why:

- Protein is highly satiating, meaning it will keep you full longer.

- Protein will help your body and muscles recover.
- Protein breaks down into amino acids, which are used by your body to create *enzymes*, which help your body carry out important chemical reactions.
- Veggies are low in calories but high in nutrients.
- Veggies will help you feel full longer without feeling heavy or needing a nap.
- Ideal veggies are high in fiber and slow to digest, improving satiety.
- Increasing vitamins and minerals midday can have a revitalizing effect on your energy.
- This lunch is easy to pack and take anywhere without requiring complicated meal prep.
- Most "lunch" foods are high in carbohydrates that decrease energy throughout the remainder of the day.
- Eating light at lunch trains your body to pull energy from stored fat to fuel the rest of your day.
- Eating light at lunch also gives you more flexibility to have a bigger and more filling dinner.

The Daily Investment

Eat only protein and veggies for lunch.

- 1-2 Chicken thighs and half a bag of baby carrots
- Deli turkey and chopped bell peppers
- Chicken salad with vinaigrette dressing

Up Your Game

As high performers, here's what we need from our lunches:

- Light enough that we don't shift into "rest and digest" mode
- High vitamins and minerals to help us stay focused and healthy
- Protein to keep us satiated and build lean muscle

So, while the chicken thighs and carrots can be an amazing way to execute on this, sometimes we're on the road and need other options.

Don't Lose Your Lunch

For that reason, it's important to have a few easy options in your back pocket so there are no excuses to miss this important Daily Investment

On the road

Even though we had a protein shake for breakfast, there is no hard and fast rule that you can't have one for lunch as well.

Only instead of adding fats, we still want to make sure you're getting the vitamins and minerals crucial to an energetic and focused afternoon.

- 2 scoops whey protein isolate
- 1 scoop powdered greens
- 2 Tbsp. powdered peanut butter
- 8 oz. Almond milk or water
    - Total carbs at lunch < 15g
    - Add ice to shake to increase satiety or make thicker
    - Add water to increase volume or thin

At a restaurant

It's easy to eat a high-protein-and-veggie lunch at a restaurant.

Even if there's not a specific menu item that looks like it fits, you can order "chicken breast and broccoli" no matter where you're at.

However, given the breadth of options, I would advise against something that boring.

I know it's obvious, but *don't* eat whatever free food they bring you before the actual food. No bread, no chips and salsa. This is garbage food that will ruin the effect you need and take you out of your ideal state during this time.

Instead, opt for:

- **Salad with protein**
  - *Add vinaigrette instead of creamy dressing*
  - *No croutons/tortilla chips*

- **Fajitas**
  - *No tortillas*

Drive-through fast food

Obviously our least favorite option, but sometimes, it happens. Whether you're on a road trip with the family or trapped with an unruly group of clients after 18 holes of golf, this can happen, and we want to be prepared.

Here are the best of the worst options:

- **Chicken salad**

  - *No croutons*
  - *No creamy dressings*

- **Breakfast burrito**
  - No potatoes
  - Dump into a bowl out of the tortilla

- **Chicken sandwich or burger in a lettuce wrap**

  - Ditch the buns

Improve your lunch

I know this section is all about how to "up your game," but the previous options are definite downgrades.

In the vein of improvement, I also like to include a few supplements at lunch time. This can provide additional vitamins and minerals when we need them as well as keep us in a health mindset.

Here are the best midday supplements you can add:

Vitamin D drops

If you did not get these in the morning, the second-best time is adding them during lunch. Limiting melatonin production can be a game-changer for staying awake on long drives or during mind-numbing projects that do not stimulate you.

Omega 3s/fish oil

Omega 3s are important for decreasing inflammation, as well as skin, hair, eye, and heart health. Most of the U.S. does not get enough of these, and gets WAY too many Omega 6s, resulting in chronic inflammation and stress.

Shoot for a brand that has at least 360mg of EPA and 240mg of DHA.

Vitamin C

Vitamin C can help keep arteries and veins healthy and elastic, which has been shown to improve longevity and energy.

Vitamin C is also critical for immune system function.

200mg per day is sufficient.

Powdered greens

Since nutrient-dense foods are important to getting the most out of our lunch, having a supplement that is densely packed with the vitamins and minerals is a great addition to a light lunch.

This should not be used in place of the veggies, but rather as a way of increasing the nutrient density of your lunch.

Have one scoop of greens in 8 ounces of water.

Sample Schedule

Here's an easy way to fit these concepts in while maintaining the integrity of the Daily Investments.

Again, these are suggestions and additions. As long as you're:

- Starting the day with 32 ounces of water and 60 seconds of explosive exercise
- Having a nutrient-dense protein shake for your first meal
- Having protein and veggies for lunch

You'll be blown away by how much focus you have and how fast fat disappears.

6:00 a.m.: Wake up
6:10 a.m.: Drink 32 oz. water
6:25 a.m.: 60 seconds of explosive exercise
6:26-7:15 a.m.: Strength training
7:15-7:20 a.m.: deep breathing and cool-down
7:20-7:30 a.m.: Cold shower and getting ready for the day
7:35 a.m.: Make and drink your protein shake
12:30 p.m.: Eat midday meal of protein and veggies

THE CEO DINNER

Most people are chronically overstressed and under recovered.

This plays out for us in different ways, from not being able to fully "turn on" when needed which reduces our focus and energy, to never being able to "turn off," which decreases our ability to restore our bodies and minds after a full day.

We live in the middle.

Average.

Neither fully engaged nor fully disconnected.

The Autonomic Nervous System (the governing systems that control all the processes going on behind the scenes in your body) has two different states. **Parasympathetic Nervous System** (PNS) dominant, and **Sympathetic Nervous System** (SNS) dominant.

When health and fitness experts talk about the Autonomic Nervous System, it's usually in reference to the PNS and within the context of *relaxing, meditating, or unwinding.*

You may also have heard of this called "rest and digest"

The antithesis to this state is the Sympathetic Nervous System (SNS) dominant. This refers to "fight or flight," which is characterized by a large adrenaline dump into your bloodstream to get away from danger.

This is what happens when we are surprised by something scary, get into a car accident, or must run away from something chasing you.

In college I signed on with a company to sell books door to door with the promise of insane riches and life experiences.

I did not know how true the latter would be.

We drove our own cars, found our own lodging, and worked our own asses off. Monday through Saturday, we started knocking at 8 a.m. and did not finish until 9:30 p.m.

My particular territory was Ashtabula County, Ohio.

One Saturday, I was following up on some leads I had not had a chance to meet with yet. It was just before 8 a.m. and I was sitting outside a house that I knew was a good prospect.

As I sat in my car listening to some jams, I noticed a neighbor walk behind my car while talking on the phone and looking at my license plate.

No big deal. Happens all the time.

I got out of the car with my permits and badges to introduce myself. Maybe sell some books. Heh.

As I left the car, he hung up the phone and started *screaming* at me. Horrible things about what he would do if he caught me in the neighborhood again, what kind of guns he had, etc. Stuff I'm not even comfortable writing out. Use your imagination.

The situation having exploded in my face, I tried to get back in the car, but he was a big dude, and I was a scrawny 19-year-old. He held me up against the car and began punching me repeatedly in the face, neck, and body.

From a biological perspective, here's what happened next:

1. My body released a large dose of adrenaline into my system.
2. My pupils dilated.
3. My body temperature shot up.
4. My blood pressure increased.
5. My breathing became rapid and shallow.
6. My digestion processes were shut off.
7. Extra blood was diverted to muscles.
8. Glucose was dumped into my bloodstream for quick energy.
9. My body burned a huge amount of stored energy.
10. Time slowed slightly as I became extremely in tune with the situation unfolding in front of me.

Here's what happened in real life:

I somehow managed to shove my assailant off me as he grabbed the badge around my neck and snapped it off.

I jumped back into my car and slammed the door on his hand as he reached in to pull me out, turned on my '97 Nissan Sentra, threw it into first gear, and took off.

I wiped the tears from my sides of my eyes with shaking hands as I tried to calm my breathing with limited success.

THIS is the definition of fight or flight. An extreme reaction to a volatile and surprising situation.

Now most of us aren't catching a beat-down on a daily basis, but we do live our lives in a state of mild SNS dominance. A low-grade stress reaction that we carry around and wear like a badge of honor.

- We don't sleep enough.
- We care too much about things that don't affect us.
- We overeat processed foods.
- We constantly worry.
- We dwell on what others think of us.
- We overuse stimulants.
- We don't consume enough of the *right* types of carbs at the *right* time.

All these factors give us low grade SNS stimulation all day, which results in cortisol (the stress hormone), lingering all day creating cravings, building belly fat, and causing premature aging.

Since the Million Dollar Body Method is predicated upon controlling our Autonomic Nervous System to reach our own personal goals, it's imperative that we learn to shut it down when necessary and ramp it up when we need the focus.

Remember, it is a spectrum. Not every stimulus is going to cause an adrenaline dump, and not every recovery technique is going to cause lethargy and paralysis.

"The dose makes the poison." -Paracelsus

That is the reason the evening meal is so critical to resetting and signaling our PNS to turn on and let us recover from the day. This PNS dominance, coupled with the correct types of food in the evening, sets us up for deeper sleep, faster.

Many people do the opposite of this technique because they have been told for years to not eat carbs after 8 p.m. or some other such nonsense.

This myth originates from a study where mice were fed a high fat diet throughout the night, when they normally would be sleeping. The mice that did not sleep, but instead at high calorie, high fat foods all night gained more weight than the control group.

Several years of selective reading and echo-chamber-fitness-blogging led us to the internet version of the child's game "telephone". "I heard from my cousin's doctor's ex-wife's personal trainer that eating carbs at night makes you fat. He read a study about it so it's definitely true."

Others do not have the flexibility to eat like this due to unscrupulous dietary choices earlier in the day.

That is why the Million Dollar Body Method is so specific about WHAT to eat, but also WHEN to eat it. By structuring daily nutrition in this way, you work with your body's natural biorhythms to create vibrant energy, and work to burn stored fat rather than training your body to rely on consumed food for daily energy.

Your body is much smarter than you or me, so working to complement the magnificent piece of machinery that we get to drive around on a daily basis is much more efficient and produces a better long-term result than forcing ourselves into a diet that relies on butter as a chief source of nutrition.

Here's What I Know:

1. Carbs help recover from training and build muscle.
2. Carbs help with "Rest and Digest" mode.
3. Eating lighter during the day gives more flexibility with family at dinner.
4. Carbs facilitate deeper sleep.

Carbs Help Recover from Training and Build Muscle

Carbohydrates are one of the main sources of fuel for our muscles. When we eat potatoes, rice, or any other carb source, it's converted into glucose after digestion and then eventually into glycogen, which is the fuel your muscles can use.

If you are not actively utilizing your body's supplies of glucose and of glycogen through training or activity, your body starts to use it to build fat.

When we work out, our muscles are forced to contract and relax repeatedly, which uses glycogen within the muscle cell for energy to produce the desired result. During the day when we are walking around, moving, and going about our daily activities, we utilize glycogen, but to a much lesser extent than during a hard training session.

Therefore, the amount of carbs we're eating should be directly proportional to the amount and intensity of the training we're doing. Completing an Ironman triathlon is going to require a lot more carbohydrates to recover and rebuild than a yoga session.

Glycogen goes hand in hand with your body's production of insulin as well. Insulin acts as a key that takes vital nutrients and unlocks the cells that those nutrients (including glycogen) belong in.

When this system is at its very best, we are:

1. Training and burning glycogen
2. Consuming the correct amount of carbohydrates, which turn into glycogen

3. Replenishing the amount of glycogen that has burned off during training sessions and throughout the day
4. Using any surplus to increase the size and density of our muscle fibers, which enables us to complete more difficult training over time

We will talk more about "training" versus "exercise" later, but suffice to say that when used properly, carbohydrates can become a delicious tool in your arsenal to help you get the results you want. It is important to recognize what carbohydrates do and how they interact with our bodies, so we know how we can manipulate them to our own gain.

Carbs Help with "Rest and Digest" Mode

When we eat a meal that is higher in carbohydrates (rice, potatoes, bread, pasta, tortillas), we get a blood-sugar spike followed by an insulin release. Our body then starts to pull energy to the gut in order to digest and process the food we just ate.

As an evolutionary response to this, our bodies shift into a parasympathetic nervous system (PNS)-dominant state, otherwise known as "rest and digest." That's why you don't feel like playing a pick-up basketball game after Thanksgiving dinner.

You do not have to understand all the chemical reactions behind this process to know that after a big meal we want to sit back, relax, and watch some football.

Rest assured, we are not about to dive into a treatise on cellular microbiology, but what we need to realize is that heavier, higher-carb meals lend themselves to feelings of relaxation and

83

slowdown. I'm pretty sure the technical term here is "chillaxing."

Although this might be obvious to you, the real magic comes from being able to create the parasympathetic "rest and digest" state on demand when it serves you and avoid that same sensation when it does not.

Eating Lighter During the Day Gives More Flexibility with Family at Dinner

One of the number one reasons many business owners and entrepreneurs tell me that they have trouble sticking to a diet is because it requires them to eat differently from their family in the evenings or cook two different meals.

Many make it two weeks, two months, or even two years with a different plan while relying solely on willpower to push through it, but eventually that becomes more expensive than the price they are willing to pay.

During this 28-day program, we are going to eat very specific foods for dinner, which your family will also enjoy.

At the end of the 28 days while you continue using MDBM frameworks in your life to create the results and energy you want; you can choose different foods to get the same results.

For example, white rice and white pasta are both fast-digesting carbs. Even though less processed food is ideal, making a simple switch to pasta or bread can be an easy way to keep your family happy while also maintaining the same structure of your nutrition that gives you the energy and the results you want.

This also can be extremely beneficial when we are going out to eat with friends, family, or for client dinners, because we will often be served some variation of this type of food and can simply select the best choice available without guilt.

Just like realizing that a song lyric you've known for a decade is in fact incorrect, once you bring awareness to how your body responds to these types of foods and how to improve upon your energy through your dinner, breakfast, and lunch, it becomes almost impossible to not have that same awareness afterward.

Carbs Facilitate Deeper Sleep

The rest and digest mode that can be gained from eating a larger meal with more carbohydrates in the evening can facilitate deeper sleep and help you get there faster. An Australian study published in the American Journal of Clinical Nutrition showed that eating a higher-carb meal four to five hours before bed can improve sleep throughout the night by increasing tryptophan and serotonin in the brain. [7]

One additional benefit this study unveiled was that having a dinner higher in carbohydrates can improve how fast you're able to fall asleep as well.

Many people report that after eating a heavy meal, they are often troubled by stomach issues or have a hard time falling asleep. Most of these issues can be traced back to rich foods, rather than high-carbohydrate foods.

Rich foods are the ones that are higher in fat that can take much longer to digest, especially those with synthetic or vegetable oils.

So, what this means is simply by eating in a way that aligns with our biology as well as what our families would probably prefer, and having a larger dinner with more delicious carbohydrates, you can improve your sleep throughout the night.

You will fall asleep faster, sleep deeper, and avoid being a diet pariah lugging around Tupperware to dinner parties.

The Objective

Eat a dinner of proteins, carbs, and veggies.

The number of great options for nutritious proteins, carbohydrates, and vegetables presents a *staggering* amount of meal options. You could easily eat different variations of these meals every night for more than 10 years without repeating a combination.

Then factor in sauces and seasonings, and the list becomes endless.

Since complexity kills momentum, we're going to focus on only three carb sources that you can combine with any protein and any vegetable, while maintaining the integrity of the program and getting a huge payoff in our results.

You will have plenty of time to explore more options after the end of the 28 days, but to give ourselves the best opportunity to discern the effects of adding in different types of foods, we must adhere to the program for the full 28 days.

No exceptions.

NOTE ON FATS: the goal is proteins, veggies, and carbs. But in cooking and serving your dinner you will generally incur a small amount of fats as well. While they are not "necessary" in this meal, the goal is simplicity and high ROI, so don't stress about them.

The general rule is fats as a garnish (bacon, avocado, cheese) or cooking aid (avocado oil, olive oil, coconut oil) are totally fine. Don't stress about them.

Stay away from foods that feature fats as a large portion of the meal though. I.e. pizza, enchiladas, alfredo sauce, etc.

Protein, carbs, and veggies for dinner is the best evening meal you can eat. Here's why:

- Protein is highly satiating, meaning it will keep you full longer.
- Protein will help your body and muscles recover.
- Protein breaks down into amino acids, which are used by your body to create *enzymes*, which help your body carry out important chemical reactions.
- Veggies are low in calories but high in nutrients.
- Carbohydrates have a recovery effect on muscles as well, especially when consumed in the final meal of the day.
- Carbohydrates take more energy to digest, helping our bodies shift into parasympathetic nervous system dominance.
- Carbs spike blood sugar and insulin, which is ideal for the end of the day when we shift toward relaxation.
- The insulin and blood sugar help to transport proteins and amino acids to muscle cells for rebuilding and growth.
- Having gone all day with lower carbs, our bodies become more insulin sensitive, leading to less stored fat.
- Carbs in the evening meal are proven to help facilitate deeper and longer sleep.
- Carbs in the evening have been shown to decrease time it takes to get to sleep.
- Carbs in the evening are ideal for a family that doesn't want to "diet."
- Most meals come in this format, so it can be easy to eat in this way at client dinners or when out with family.
- This framework is easy to follow at other people's houses, picnics, BBQs, and other times when you don't have your ideal food available.

- Eating lighter all day provides a bit of leniency for dinner.
- Carbs can include fruit or other treats, which allows dessert.

The Daily Investment

Eat a dinner of meat, veggies, and either rice potatoes, or sweet potatoes.

Here are 3 options using the best possible carbs. Obviously, these can be changed or tweaked, but start with some simple options before branching out.

1. Slow-cooked pork carnitas with baked potato

3-4-lb. pork loin (or preferred cut)
1 Tbsp. each of cumin, coriander, oregano, and salt
1 cup water with bouillon/ broth
2 bay leaves
1 diced onion
1/2 can of chipotle chili peppers (5 or 6 peppers)
3-4 russet potatoes

Directions:

Combine everything except potatoes in slow cooker and cook on low for 8-10 hours.

Bake potatoes in oven for 30 min. at 450 degrees or poke holes in them and heat in microwave for 10 min.

2. Sweet potato pasta with meatballs and Brussel sprouts

3-5 sweet potatoes spiralized (you need a spiralizer to make this easy)
6-8 meatballs per person (frozen is great)

1 jar sugar-free spaghetti sauce
1 lb. Brussel sprouts (you can sub this for any other veg)

Directions:

Heat oven to 450.

Spiralize the potatoes and put on a baking sheet.

Cut Brussel sprouts in half and put on baking sheet.

Put meatballs on baking sheet.

Put avocado oil, salt, and pepper on potatoes and sprouts and put everything in oven.

(Note: Brussel sprouts need about 20 min, while the potatoes can need closer to 30.)

Heat sauce in a pan and add meatballs when they are done heating.

3. Taco bowl

1-2 C white rice (dry)
1 bag frozen cut bell peppers (Trader Joes)
1 lb. lean ground beef (cook with taco seasoning.)
1 can black beans
1-2 tomatoes, diced

Directions:

Put rice in a rice cooker. White rice needs a 2:3 ratio of rice to water.

Cook the beef first. Add taco seasoning to taste.

Add beans and bell peppers together in a skillet. Simmer for 5-10 min.

Add on top of rice and romaine lettuce or eat as a standalone dish. Season with salsa, avocado, or hot sauce.

Up Your Game

With breakfast and lunch being the most strict and controlled meals, we have more options and opportunities at dinner.

We're focusing on only three main types of carbs as a part of the Million Dollar Body Method because potatoes and rice are easy to digest and give us exactly the reaction we're looking for. They increase blood sugar and insulin response while facilitating deeper sleep.

Neither has additional components that could interact poorly with digestion and most people are not allergic to either, which make them perfect for this program.

Plus, potatoes and rice are delicious and can be turned into a limitless number of dishes.

Improve your dinner with gratitude

Praying before meals or otherwise showing gratitude for what you are about to enjoy has been shown to improve digestion, trigger PNS activation, and help you enjoy your meal more.

Even if you do not pray, simply being grateful for the food, and making your *intention* that this dinner will nourish your body and provide deep sleep will help bring those benefits to fruition.

Not sure what to say?

Try: "*I am grateful for the healthy and nutritious food I am about to consume. I know this food will help me continue to build a healthy body and will facilitate a night of deep, restorative sleep.*"

Add dessert

Maybe this is not upping your game, but some people get a sweet tooth after dinner. And rather than fight it, let us continue to use the principles described in this book to get the benefits rather than guilt.

Having a dessert that fuels you is simple. We want to make sure we have protein along with our carbs, while not going out of our way to add any fats. Having some is no problem, but do not add

Rich, fatty foods will keep you from sleeping as well.

Here are two good options:

1. Yogurt parfait

3/4 C Greek yogurt
1/3 scoop whey protein isolate (whip it up good for best results)
1/2 cup fruit (banana, berries, pineapple)

2. Cottage cheese and fruit

1 C cottage cheese
1/2 cup fruit (banana, berries, pineapple)

Sample Schedule

Here's an easy way to fit these concepts in while maintaining the integrity of the Daily Investments.

These are suggestions and additions. As long as you're:

- Starting the day with 32 ounces of water and 60 seconds of explosive exercise
- Having a nutrient-dense protein shake for your first meal
- Having protein and veggies for lunch

- Having protein, veggies, and rice or potatoes for dinner

You'll be blown away by how much focus you have and how fast fat disappears.

6:00 a.m.: Wake up
6:10 a.m.: Drink 32 oz. water
6:25 a.m.: 60 seconds of explosive exercise
6:26-7:15 a.m.: Strength training
7:15-7:20 a.m.: deep breathing and cool-down
7:20-7:30 a.m.: Cold shower and getting ready for the day
7:35 a.m.: Make and drink your protein shake
12:30 p.m.: Midday meal of protein and veggies
6:30 p.m.: Dinner of protein, veggies, and potato/rice
7:30 p.m.: Dessert of yogurt parfait

DAILY INVESTMENT 5:

FINAL DEPOSIT

Have you ever had the night where you know you have something first thing in the morning, and whether through poor planning, or overconfidence in your own abilities you don't set an alarm clock?

Recently I had left my phone in the car, and just decided not to get it before going to bed. I had something to do where I needed to be up by 7am, which is normal for me.

So, no need to set an alarm, right?

You probably know where this is going.

Instead of a restful night of sleep where I was awakened to the luxurious sounds of my iPhone's alarm clock, I woke up and checked my watch at 1 am...

Then 2 a.m...
3:45 a.m...
5:15 a.m...
5:45 a.m...

...and again at 6:20 a.m., when I then was able to get my deepest, most restful sleep of the night before waking up at 7:15 am and losing my mind trying to dress, brush my teeth and grab some food to leave the house in under three minutes.

Many of us can relate to this.

2 in every 5 Americans get less than 7 hours of sleep per night. 70% of Americans report at least one night per month is spent tossing and turning, and 11% of people report sleeping poorly every night. [11]

Insomnia and sleep apnea are serious medical issues, but the majority of us suffer from hyperactive brains, day-to-day stress, and future worry.

If there was a way you could guarantee that you would be able to eliminate the thoughts, worries, and ruminations that keep you from falling asleep or staying that way, would you do it? What would you pay for something that kept your brain from running amok as you are trying to nod off?

Luckily for us, there is an easy solution to this problem. And it does not cost a dime.

The Secret Weapon

There is a book that came out in 2006 that caused a hubbub in the personal development community.

Written by Rhonda Byrne, some people swore by the teachings in the book, while some said it was meaningless fluff.

The book was called The Secret. Maybe you've heard of it.

The premise of the book is the "law of attraction." Basically, what you think about and visualize will come to pass in your life.

Regardless of how you feel about the book or the premise that the more you think about Pokémon, the better chance you have of catching a Pikachu (this never worked for me tbh), it does hit on an extremely specific aspect of our brains that we can use to our advantage.

This piece of hardware is called the "Reticular Activating System" (RAS). It is a grouping of neurons in the brain that help mediate behavior.

In practicality, this small piece of hardware describes the sensation you get when you buy a car and suddenly start noticing the same style of car on the road around you all the time.

For example, my wife purchased a bright orange Honda Fit that she lovingly named, *"The Mystic Turd."* I never knew how many of these cars were out there, but as I write this, I exist in a world fully populated by Mystic Turds.

Taking this one step further, the RAS is also the reason that some people who complain all the time seem to have such shit luck while people who visualize their goals and dreams seem to check off box after box in pursuit of success.

Simply, the RAS is the conduit between *awareness* and *energy*.

The more time you spend ruminating on a topic or opportunity, the more ways you're going to come up with to solve it. You will suddenly have a brilliant idea in the shower, or while driving or doing something completely unrelated. Putting awareness and intention on a task can cause your RAS to sniff out answers like a bloodhound.

That's why this simple task is so important and provides a huge ROI.

By writing just 3 lines every night before bed, we set our subconscious on a path to find solutions as well as alleviate the burden that lingering tasks put on our short-term memory if not relegated to their proper places.

Here's What I Know:

1. Writing down objectives eliminates rumination.
2. Rituals lead to better results
3. The easiest way to ensure a solid night's rest is to have a reason to wake up in the morning.

Writing Down Objectives Eliminates Rumination

When we can take what's in our brain, write it down, take a breath, and then set down our pen, it gives us the ability to turn off some of those persistent thoughts.

This works because our brains recognize that we've done all we can toward fulfilling goals or eliminating worries, and no longer need to rely on short-term memory to keep them top of mind.

If you are like the 62% of Americans that report not being able to fall asleep when they lay down, there's a good probability it's because you're thinking too much about the past or planning too hard for the future, both of which you have no control over.

By taking our plans, goals, desires, and problems, and writing them down, we give our brain permission to shut off and start relying on the notepad for memory. This also facilitates the transfer from short-term memory to subconscious.

Our brains crave finality and action. They desperately want to scratch the itch of solving a problem that bothers us. When we take the first step of writing down whatever that problem is, our brains see this as being "good enough," and are then allowed to move on and start processing other tasks.

Robert Louis Stevenson, author of Treasure Island and The Strange Case of Dr Jekyll and Mr. Hyde, used this principle with a great degree of success over the course of his career.

He was convinced that his subconscious (which he called his "brownies") would whisper the plots of his famous books into his ear while he slept. He would simply write down some notes for himself or set the intention of creating a fantastic story, and then would wake up with the answers he desired.

Even though we might not be writers or creators, simply by writing down what needs doing, we can set our subconscious to the task of solving these problems behind the scenes as we sleep.

Rituals Lead to Better Results

By installing a positive ritual in your evening, you will start training your body and brain to sleep better during the night.

This can be writing down three to five problems to tackle tomorrow, or it can be something as simple as pulling down a sleep mask over your eyes after you finish reading.

If the rituals are simple, structured, and repeated at the same time daily, these can cue our body and brain in on the fact that there is an expectation that follows the act of writing, brushing our teeth, or taking specific supplements.

An added benefit of writing three things down for tomorrow is the ability to utilize your Reticular Activating System to be more aware and pay attention to the exact steps you need to take to have a very productive day tomorrow.

By continuing to write down your critical tasks in the evening, throughout the night and next day you will get the added benefit of your brain seeking out solutions, even in places you might not have thought to look.

The Easiest Way to Ensure a Solid Night's Rest is to Have a Reason to Wake Up in the Morning

When we finish the day on a positive note having accomplished something, it is one of the most satisfying feelings in the world.

When we can manufacture this feeling on demand, we sleep deeper and feel more content and successful.

By writing down the three things you need to accomplish the following day, you are finalizing the day on a positive note because you are finishing out everything you can possibly do in the moment.

This also takes all residual information that requires short-term memory power, and puts it down on paper, thus freeing up your brain to fully shift into a parasympathetic state.

The short-term memory is limited to roughly five to nine "slots". With everything you are doing on a daily basis, there are a lot of different activities competing for your attention. Most entrepreneurs average about 50 items all simultaneously asking for attention.

The best move here is to take those competing thoughts and move them over to an external source of "memory" that can do it better. Using the tools we have available will free our memory and brain power up to take action on the important steps, rather than what type of dog food we need to pick up at the store.

This also creates extreme clarity on the steps that need to be taken in the morning to ensure a positive day.

Completing this process allows us to go to sleep with a sense of calm and wake up with clarity and conviction. All of that in less than five minutes as a part of your nighttime routine.

The Objective

Write down your top three critical tasks for the following day.

You can have more or less than 3, but the goal is to scribe your most important undertakings for the following day, which, if checked off, would cause you to look at the day as a success.

Some days there is only one main thing.

Some days feel like there are 10 or more. On days like that, write down the whole list, and then go back and cross off what you deem to be less important after taking the time to get *everything* out of your head.

You can do this in a note in your phone, but I prefer a pad and paper kept on the nightstand. There is something more visceral about writing out each task by hand, and it feels more satisfying to cross off each one.

Writing out your three critical tasks is magic. Here's why:

- No more relying on memory. It is written down and therefore impossible to forget.
- No burdening your short-term memory with tasks it is not suited for, which can result in restless sleep and feelings of anxiety.

- This simple act reduces worry by coalescing your problems into three tasks, rather than a nebulous amount of "stuff" for the following day.
- When you write these down, you allow your subconscious to take over and dream up solutions that your conscious mind may have overlooked.
- Having a nighttime ritual can lead to better sleep because your brain and body are cued that sleep follows this task.
- Waking up in the morning is easier if you have a mission to accomplish.

The Daily Investment

Write down your three critical tasks for tomorrow before bed.

Up Your Game

You might already have an evening routine that is more in-depth than this or includes some version of the critical three.

If so, that's great. If it is working for you, don't change it.

If you have some more time or want to add additional components that can help you process your day and prepare for the day tomorrow, here are some of the best practices you can add in.

PM Prep for an Amazing Day

Supplements

As you finish your critical three, take some zinc and magnesium. They will help with hormonal health, recovery, and deeper sleep.

Magnesium taurinate or gluconate is better than the cheaper version of magnesium oxide.

Read something motivational

Read something that puts you in the headspace of what you're going to accomplish the next day.

If improving health and fitness is your goal, read more about that (n8trainingsystems.com/ has you covered).

If you need to improve your leadership abilities at work, perhaps Extreme Ownership by Jocko Willink is your next book.

If you're working on parenting....well, you get it.

Highly addictive fiction books are a slippery slope, though. One minute you are tired and picking up a book for a few pages, and two hours later you're wondering how Harry Potter is going to get out of the current mess he's found himself in.

Meditate

There are a lot of different ways to meditate, but in the evening, I prefer guided meditation on an app, or simply listening to some meditative music while focusing on deep, diaphragmatic breathing.

Any way you decide to do this is great; even starting with a few minutes can provide benefits. A new study showed that all it takes is 11 hours of meditation over several weeks to change the way your brain is wired, and to improve focus and the ability to concentrate. [8]

Journaling

Simply writing down your thoughts, wins, goals, problems, or even what you did during the day can be extremely beneficial for offloading some of the worries we hold with us.

By writing out our goals daily, we can also cue our Reticular Activation System (RAS) to stay focused on the things that matter most to us.

Gratitude

A phenomenal way to rewire our brain is to constantly seek out and express things we are grateful for.

Whether it is simply praying and being thankful for a roof over our heads, clean water, or something more involved like writing a note to someone you appreciate, there are millions of opportunities to be grateful every day.

Writing out one or more of the things you are grateful for is an excellent way to improve your perspective and outlook.

Here's an easy way to fit these concepts in while maintaining the integrity of the Daily Investments.

These are suggestions and additions. As long as you're:

- Starting the day with 32 ounces of water and 60 seconds of explosive exercise
- Having a nutrient-dense protein shake for your first meal
- Having protein and veggies for lunch
- Having protein, veggies, and rice or potatoes for dinner
- Writing down your critical 3 for tomorrow

You'll be blown away by how much focus you have and how fast fat disappears.

6:00 a.m.: Wake up
6:10 a.m.: Drink 32 oz. water
6:25 a.m.: 60 seconds of explosive exercise
6:26-7:15 a.m.: Strength training
7:15-7:20 a.m.: Deep breathing and cool down
7:20-7:30 a.m.: Cold shower and getting ready for the day
7:35 a.m.: Make and drink your protein shake
12:30 p.m.: Midday meal of protein and veggies
6:30 p.m.: Dinner of protein, veggies, and potato/rice
7:30 p.m.: Dessert of yogurt parfait
9:30 p.m.: Write down your critical three for tomorrow

DAILY INVESTMENT 6:

LIQUID ASSETS

You obviously already know that water is important. In case you forgot from Daily Investment 1, here is that piece of breaking news again:

YOU NEED TO DRINK MORE WATER.

Dehydration is a killer of focus, a purveyor of hunger, and completely preventable. To be suffering from dehydration in a country that has more bottled water brands than NFL teams is ludicrous.

Especially when you consider that the U.S. tap water is safe to drink and can quench your thirst equally as well as that $5 bottle of alkaline water.

We know all the facts about water and dehydration. But here's something you might not know: Water is necessary for the process of fat loss.

Crucial.

Here are the basics:

The average human stores between 60,000 and 100,000 calories of energy in their body fat cells.

When we "burn fat," we do not just break down the cells and get rid of them. Instead, there is a chemical reaction that "empties" the cell of the fat and turns it into Free Fatty Acids (FFAs).

To clear the fat out of the cell, a reaction called HYDROlysis must take place where water is added to the fat cell first, REPLACING the fat in the cell, and allowing it to break down into the more bioavailable FFAs.

The FFAs are then whisked through your bloodstream where they are used for energy in the mitochondria of muscle cells (remember high school biology?)

This means that the MORE hydrated you are, the MORE fat you're able to liberate, and the MORE your muscles will be able to use that fat for energy. [9]

Hydration is crucial if you want to burn fat.

After this process takes place, over the next few days, the water empties from the cell, leaving you with smaller, unfilled fat cells, which will give you the lean, healthy appearance you're looking for.

I had a client who could not stand water.

He said he got bloated easily, and he did not want to take in more fluids and increase the bloat. I kept telling him that regular water would do the opposite, by helping eliminate fluid retention.

He hemmed and hawed, but no matter what, he would not drink enough. Eventually we quit working together and I had not seen him in a few months.

One Thursday we got together for lunch, and he looked great! His face looked less bloated, and you could see his chest through his shirt, rather than his gut sticking out.

He was also grinning like a maniac, so I knew something was up.

He told me, "I eventually got so fed up with how I looked and how tired I always felt, so I decided to do what you said and have a gallon of water every day for a week, just to see.

"After a few days, I couldn't believe it. My head felt clearer, and I dropped 3 lbs., but felt like I had dropped closer to 10! Plus, drinking water is no big deal anymore"

Our bodies are very smart and tend to take what they need. So, if you're not drinking enough water, your body will hold on to what you are giving it, which can lead to bloating, feeling distended, or the appearance of cellulite.

When you rehydrate and give your body the water it needs for all its important processes, it can let go of the stored water and use what you give it through drinking.

There are a lot of high-level chemical reactions that need water taking place in your body and brain thousands of times per minute. But you do not need to be a biologist to know that you need to stay hydrated.

So, before you spend a lot of money on a cleanse or fancy supplements, make sure you're getting enough water first.

Here's What I Know:

1. Hydration is critical to health.

2. 75% of Americans are chronically dehydrated.
3. You can supercharge your brain with proper hydration.
4. More hydration equals more fat burn.

Hydration is Critical to Physical Health

Drinking the right amount of water each day is crucial to your health and longevity. Water:

- Regulates your body temperature
- Makes sure your joints stay lubricated
- Delivers nutrients to cells
- Helps burn body fat
- Keeps your brain, your eyes, and your organs functioning properly
- Decreases the prevalence of disease
- Boosts your energy
- Improve your metabolism
- Keeps tendons and ligaments more elastic
- Delivers oxygen through your body
- Keeps skin looking young
- Keeps spine healthy
- Naturally detoxifies your body
- Flushes waste

Water is required for almost 100% of the chemical reactions that take place in your body. Whether it is your organs functioning properly, the process of autophagy, (the clearing out of old and broken-down cells) or facilitating the fat loss process, water plays an integral part in each procedure.

Water makes up almost 70% of each human's body on the planet. Because of the necessity of H_2O in everything we do, we are losing water all the time through simple chemical reactions that do not get our attention: Going to the bathroom, sweating, breathing, and even the process of blinking to keep our eyes lubricated.

As we age, our fluid reserves become smaller and our ability to conserve water is decreased. Older humans also become less sensitive to the sensation of thirst, which can play into increased sensations of hunger, even when we do not necessarily need food.

75% of Americans are Chronically Dehydrated

Even though most Americans get roughly eight servings of fluids per day, the majority of those are coming from coffee or soda, which are net neutral when it comes to hydration because of their diuretic effects.

Dehydration is also commonly to blame for intense feelings of fatigue during exercise and even when sedentary. Dehydration is the number one cause of midday fatigue in adults.

Chronic dehydration can lead to kidney stones, kidney failure, cramps, heat exhaustion, seizures, or even low blood-volume shock.

Dehydration increases your skin's vulnerability to disorders and disease, and can cause headaches, bloating, and stomach cramps.

When dehydrated, we are also at risk of hunger pangs or cravings because our bodies are no longer attuned to the sensation of thirst, and we mistake it for hunger extremely often. This leads to a vicious cycle of eating more, spending more energy digesting food, and further increasing our water debt.

Dehydration also is linked to having worse memory, being irritable, or having dips in concentration and focus throughout the day. Worse, anytime we feel the sensation of being thirsty, it means we are *already* dehydrated.

Dehydration can come from something as simple as a 1-2% decrease in the amount of fluids you need. But crazy enough, a decrease of 3% of cellular hydration can be linked to up to a 30% decrease in strength. This means that if you're 3% dehydrated, your bench press of 200 pounds is now going to be pushing 140.

Supercharge Your Brain with Proper Hydration

My aunt always got headaches in the middle of the day, no matter how much caffeine she had and no matter if she took Advil or not, she always had a constant low-grade headache that would drive her nuts.

She asked me for help with two issues: More energy in the afternoons and mitigating the headaches that set in around 2 p.m. At first, nothing worked. We could not figure out the cause. It was not sugar or caffeine withdrawal or a diet in rich and fatty foods. It was not until we started tracking her water intake that we noticed she didn't drink any water between 8 a.m. and 5 p.m. She drank other things — energy drinks, coffee, or tea — but no water by itself.

When we simply started tracking the water more effectively and putting a high priority on getting more water and less caffeine, her energy instantly improved and best of all, her headaches went away.

At the same time, she started training more frequently because of feeling better, and the weight magically started melting off as well.

Oftentimes, headaches and other body or brain issues are the body's way of telling us we are out of balance. By getting back into balance, we can turn off these negative "signals" from our body while improving focus and mental cognition, as well as supercharging short-term memory — an invaluable skill to an entrepreneur.

Water gives your brain access to the vitamins, minerals, and nutrients it needs daily. Because of the way our brain works, being properly hydrated can increase the speed of synaptic responses, which means you can think and respond quicker, especially in higher-stress situations.

And water, more than any other compound in the world, can boost your physical and mental performance during training. If you are dehydrated, nothing can help you, but if you're properly hydrated, you can get much more out of performance-enhancing compounds and nootropics.

As a bonus, water is also a key component of eliminating and avoiding hangovers, as the main causes are dehydration and a lack of vitamins and minerals.

More Hydration Equals More Fat Burn

Obviously, water is calorie-free. So, anytime you have a chance to replace a calorie-laden beverage like fruit juices, creamy coffees, or alcohol with water, you are going to be mitigating calorie intake.

Studies have also shown that people who primarily stick to water eat 9% less than those who do not.

But one of the most fascinating things about water as it relates to fat loss is how we burn fat. Many people think that burning fat happens on the treadmill in the gym, when in fact training does *not* burn fat.

If anything, doing longer bouts of cardio can burn muscle. So, when we are training, we don't need a fat-burn effect in that moment. The goal is to burn glycogen (muscle energy), but then have a body that has been trained to pull from stored energy (fat cells) to rebuild and repair our muscles and tissues over the next 48 hours.

Read that again.

When we sleep, we start to expel fat, and our body goes through a complex chemical process that we described earlier where fat cells are emptied out of their contents, but refilled with water, and this process **cannot** take place if you are chronically dehydrated.

As a side note, this is often why the scale does not accurately reflect how much weight we've lost day to day because our fat cells can be filled with liquid during the process of fat loss.

As we sleep and exhale moist air, that is where we are expelling our fat. It is not burning off when we sweat, or when we use the bathroom. Instead, it is being breathed out at night as we sleep.

This is why being hydrated is one of the daily investments we must focus on if we want to feel focused, look awesome, and have our ideal amount of energy.

Chronic dehydration is a recipe for being unable to burn fat and can leave you feeling fatigued, hungry, lethargic, achy, and frustrated with the lack of results.

It's yet another reason to start our day with 32 ounces of water, so that way we're not playing catch up in the evening, which can knock us out of a deep sleep in order to get up and use the bathroom.

A single-minded focus on the Million Dollar Body Method, exactly how it is laid out, is going to give you the best possible results.

The Objective

Drink one gallon of water every day.

Does everyone need to drink exactly 128 ounces of water? No.

The amount of water you need is individual, and changes based on activity level, fatigue, caffeine ingestion, where you live, the season, and a host of other factors.

But most of us need 100+ ounces, and do not get anywhere close to that.

One gallon is a great starting point, and for this program, we are going to focus on hitting that on a daily basis to ensure we have enough to make our focus and fat loss automatic.

Drinking enough water is crucial to looking and feeling your best. Here's why:

- It can improve your metabolism and help you digest food more effectively.
- It will keep you from feeling hungry throughout the day as the body often mistakes thirst for hunger.
- Water lubricates your joints and helps your muscles work better.
- Water facilitates fat loss as you sleep.
- The more water you drink, the less you will store as bloat.

- Water helps you focus better by fueling your brain.
- Water will "detoxify" your body and use your natural systems to remove waste. No cleanse required.
- Water improves your skin's appearance.
- Water improves how well your body systems function.
- Not enough water can cause headaches, joint pains, and digestive issues.

The Daily Investment

Drink one gallon of water per day.

In an ideal world, we would frontload the start of your day in order to keep you from getting up at night to pee.

That is why we start the day with ¼ of the water up front. If you have another 32 ounces mid-morning, and another 32 after lunch, you are on the right track.

Up Your Game

There are a lot of ways to improve your water consumption, but none of them include "adding Crystal Light" to your H_2O.

Instead, think of it as a micro-cleanse for your body every time you finish another glass of water.

Add Vitamin D drops to your water

As we already talked about with the morning routine, adding some Vitamin D to your morning water is a great way to start the day with a bit more energy, improve your immune system, and stay in a healthy mindset all day.

Add lemon before meals

Adding lemon to your water can be done in the morning, but one easy way to improve is by having a glass of water with the juice of half a lemon in it before meals.

Not only does this add in a few additional times of the day where you can have another glass of water — making it easier to hit the gallon mark — adding lemon can improve digestion as well.

Lemon will stimulate your body's natural production of hydrochloric acid (HCL), which can help you break down your meals and improve digestion. If you find that you are gassy after eating, this can be a game-changer for you (and everyone around you).

Sea salt

For those of us who are highly active or who train more than 5 hours per week, adding some sea salt to your water post workout or before bed can be great for replenishing electrolytes.

If you find that you wake up to pee a lot during the night, adding some salt to your water before bed can keep this from happening. Start with ¼ teaspoon and work up to a full teaspoon over a week.

Water and walk

Another way to combine great habits is by drinking a glass of water before you go out for a quick walk, or every time you stand up from your desk.

If your job has you pinned to a chair for large chunks of time, set a timer for every 50 minutes to remind yourself to stand up and stretch, and while you do that, have a glass of water as well.

Remember: If you are feeling thirsty, you're already dehydrated.

The rubber band trick

One easy way to track your water throughout the day is by getting a 32-ounce water bottle and putting 4 rubber bands at the top.

Every time you finish a bottle, move one of the rubber bands from the top to the bottom, so you know by the end of the day that you got the full amount.

Sample Schedule

Here's an easy way to fit these concepts in while maintaining the integrity of the Daily Investments.

These are suggestions and additions. As long as you're:

- Starting the day with 32 ounces of water and 60 seconds of explosive exercise
- Having a nutrient-dense protein shake for your first meal
- Having protein and veggies for lunch
- Having protein, veggies, and rice or potatoes for dinner
- Writing down your critical 3 for tomorrow
- Drinking one gallon of water per day

You'll be blown away by how much focus you have and how fast fat disappears.

6:00 a.m.: Wake up
6:10 a.m.: Drink 32 oz. water

6:25 a.m.: 60 seconds of explosive exercise
6:30-7:15 a.m.: Strength training + **water**
7:15-7:20 a.m.: Deep breathing and cooldown
7:20-7:30 a.m.: Cold shower and getting ready for the day
7:35 a.m.: Make and drink your protein shake
12:30 p.m.: Eat midday meal of protein and veggies + **water**
6:30 p.m.: Dinner of protein, veggies, and potato/rice + **water**

DAILY INVESTMENT 7:

WORK HARD, TRAIN HARDER

Train (verb). To develop and improve a mental or physical faculty through instruction or practice.

F rom our favorite sports icons, musicians, artists, and even the heroes of our favorite movie franchises, the people we look up to *train*.

Michael Jordan shot 3s long into the night after his teammates went home.

Navy SEALs endure unfathomable pain and discomfort to train their bodies and minds to push through any situation.

Pianist John Burke writes music that is too difficult for him to play, then trains to improve by practicing it slowly until he's able to play at full speed.

Copywriting legend Gary C. Halbert trains his skills by transcribing by hand other masterful copywriting.

Training is key to success if you want to be the best.

History is also littered with the names of big-time athletes who had all the talent in the world, but lack of discipline and training led to disappointing careers.

Training is simply the act of working to improve a skill or trait through practice. This definition has little in common with what most people consider when they talk about exercise.

Training requires constant improvement and tracking progress, not a half-assed session on the elliptical.

Training means that you are competing against your past successes, not randomly deciding to max out on bench press so the hottie stretching in the corner notices your gains.

Training makes you disciplined; exercise makes you sweaty.

That is why this Daily Investment is training, not exercise. It necessitates that you will have improved in the 28 days of this program, not merely gotten sweaty 28 times.

And while there is nothing wrong with exercise, movement, and getting sweaty, to fully embrace the idea of training requires you to become MORE, rather than how we normally talk about weight *loss, dropping* fat, slimming *down,* etc.

Physical training can be done in myriad ways.

You can run, bike, swim, do calisthenics, lift heavy weights, box, jump rope, or a plethora of other options.

The thing that separates training from exercising is consistent improvement.

Whether that is tracking your weights over time as you work to improve your physique and strength in the gym, focusing on becoming faster and cleaner with your left hook, or running slightly farther in the time allotted, the goal is improvement.

And we cannot know what our improvement is without tracking.

Don't overcomplicate this, either. Many of us will start a new plan and then find ourselves doing hours of research to find the "best" workout program or trying to write our own that helps us get bigger, leaner, stronger, and faster all at once.

A better option would be to run for 20 minutes and work on increasing distance each time.

Or do as many pushups, squats, and pullups as you can in that time.

Or give yourself 20 minutes every day to practice difficult calisthenics like L sits and headstands.

You can also go to n8trainingsystems.com/MDBMtraining to get my recommended gym or home training program that goes perfectly with the Million Dollar Body Method.

Again, the goal is consistent, daily improvement.

Consistent Daily Improvement is a rarity.

- It allows us the space to "grind" on a particular task until we see progress.
- It teaches us that the obstacle is the way.

- It shows us that we are limitless, given enough focus and time.
- It provides a forced meditation and singular focus.
- It builds confidence *every* time a session is completed.

Training is a time that we get to experience the magic of rote repetition and boredom. If we can push through the spot where our brains are telling us to do something different, growth and improvement waits for us on the other side.

Even though training montages are exciting, and feature a ripped dude sweating his ass off flipping tires in the desert to a hip-hop soundtrack, that's not the truth of it.

Anyone who has trained for a marathon, a fight, or a competition will tell you that training can get boring. But the success you are looking for is just on the other side. Once you hit it, get excited, because that is where the magic happens.

This is also true from a physiological perspective. The first few weeks of attempting a new workout program, learning to swing a golf club, or working on a new punch combination, most of the improvement takes place in your brain.

These neurological adaptations can lead to strength gains as your brain is rewired to give you more ability in whatever technique you were learning. But as neurological gains taper off around Week 3, that is when the physical changes start taking place.

Many people never get to this point, which is why their bodies look the same year after year despite going to the gym.

That's why boot camps, or constantly varied movements that focus on making you sweaty (I'm looking at you, burpees) make such a minimal impact on the bodies of participants. They confuse "tired" for "trained."

Average people who do average work get average results.

We are not average.

Here's What I Know:

1. Nutrition causes weight loss, training changes your body
2. Training improves your ability to handle stress
3. Training builds discipline
4. Training creates more energy

Nutrition Causes Weight Loss. Training Changes Your Body

When you lose a lot of weight through excessive amounts of cardio or focus on nutrition at the exclusion of any sort of resistance training or physical adaptations, you will lose fat.

But you're neglecting a large number of benefits that can be gained from training your body to improve.

Without training, fat loss can lead to becoming a smaller version of your previous self. This is what is known as "skinny fat."

This is another reason that people who go on extreme weight-loss diets, do the HCG protocol, get a lap band, or even engage in marathon and extreme distance running do not necessarily have muscular physiques. Because they are training their bodies to maintain a stored fat level that can help them stay alive.

The body is incredibly intelligent. Think of it as being run by a sophisticated team of engineers who react to all the inputs that we put in daily, whether from nutrition, training, the news we watch or the pharmaceuticals we take.

Our bodies continually adapt to the stimulus we put in. When we start decreasing calories to burn fat or try any other extreme dietary measures, our body does not understand that we are doing this to lose weight.

Our body is resistant to change. Therefore, it sees weight loss as a threat to our longevity and health. In order to continue to keep us alive, it will start eliminating non-essential daily functions.

If you are a "toe tapper," your body will eliminate the need to tap your feet because it considers that a non-essential use of calories. People find that they sit more and use less energy overall.

This leads to a vicious cycle of your body using less calories, which slows down your metabolic rate. So, while you are eating less, you're also burning less and suppressing your metabolism over time.

On the other hand, when we use some form of training to actively change our body, we are giving the input that we need more strength and muscle mass to do more, and our body's engineers react accordingly to give us the adaptations to stay alive.

Think about it like this: Two guys need 2,000 calories to survive without gaining any weight on a daily basis, and both want to change the way they look and feel.

Guy #1 drops his calories to 1,500 and does not change any of his daily activities. Over time, his metabolism will decrease to the point where he only needs 1,600 calories to maintain his new physique. This means he must continue to eat a low-calorie diet to maintain results.

However, if he is still 10 pounds overweight, it's more difficult now to drop his calories even further to get results. Making someone like that eat 1,200 calories or fewer is a great way to suppress hormones, decrease testosterone, drop energy, and generally be hungry all the time.

Guy #2, rather than decreasing his calories, simply increases his energy expenditure through training by 300 to 500 calories per day. He incorporates resistance training, walking, and hill sprints, to become more fit and athletic.

Guy #2 is now instructing his body to take the food he's eating and put it toward recovery from training as well as gaining lean muscle. Over time, his metabolism goes from needing 2,000 calories to 2,200 to maintain that new lean muscle. Now he is able to eat more and has a physique and the metabolism to match.

Which would you prefer?

Training Improves Your Ability to Handle Stress

Training, cardio, and even yoga is actually a *stressor* for your body. It requires your body to go into a sympathetic nervous system dominant state: fight or flight. It releases cortisol, a stress hormone, and it can cause your body to need to recover longer, especially after exceedingly difficult sessions.

By doing this in a controlled environment where we can match our training with our recovery, we are able to condition our body to what is called *eustress*, or positive stress. The more we train our bodies to handle eustress, the better we get at managing *distress*, the negative version many people feel every day.

Training also increases endorphin output in the brain. Endorphins are positive brain chemicals that can alter your mood. They can help you feel better, think faster, and give you a more positive outlook on life.

Even though training in itself is a stress, it also mitigates the effects of stress you feel from other areas of life. Much like mindfulness, when you are singularly focused on a specific task, like being under the bar for a heavy squat, it is very difficult to think about an email that you should have sent or something your boss did at work that's pissing you off.

Training is also much like meditation in this way. It is a forced focus on one task to the exclusion of everything else. Anyone who has done a heavy set of 20 squats or used the rower for a timed set can tell you, it's very difficult to focus on anything else besides your breathing and the exercise at hand while you're pushing yourself to your maximum output.

This is a physical type of meditation that can be a highly effective way to meditate for those of us who have trouble sitting still in the dark.

Training Builds Discipline

Training mimics everything that is difficult in life. When I was in high school, I was on the track team. I ran the 400m and did pole vault. Standing at 6-foot-4 and 155 pounds, I did not necessarily have the body type that would break any records, but I always had fun and tried hard.

One day, I overhead the vault coach talking to the sprint coach. He was upset at the general lack of talent from our squad and said something I will not soon forget. "*I'm not even gonna bring these guys to the city meet. They'll embarrass themselves. Normally, pole vaulters should be the studliest guys on the team."*

He pointed out one of the bigger, faster, stronger guys who also played quarterback at our school. *"You think I could borrow him for a season so we could actually have a shot?"*

I remember thinking, "Wow, that really sucks."

The next day, I went to my guidance counselor and I asked if I could switch out one of my classes for a weight training class instead. From that point on, I started going to the gym to gain the muscle and strength that I thought would finally get people to respect me.

What I didn't realize is that in my quest for bulky muscles, I got so much more.

After a year or so with lackluster results because I designed a plan myself as a high school senior (arms, chest, abs and arms, chest and arms, biceps), the thought that started to crystalize for me was that no matter how long it took me, I was going to get the results I wanted, and I was going to achieve the goal I'd set for myself.

This was great as it applied to fitness and health, and I now can say that I look and feel the way I want to look and feel.

But, even more powerful from a discipline perspective, I can now confidently say that if I set my mind to something, no matter how long it takes, I will make it to those goals because it is not possible to lose if you never quit.

> "You just can't beat the person that never gives up." - Babe Ruth

Taking that mentality to the rest of your life is so much more powerful than having a big bench press or awesome biceps.

For every 10 workouts you do, one is going to be amazing and you are going to feel like Superman. One is going to suck and you're going to feel like absolute dog shit. Eight of them are going to be fine, but it is in those eight boring, average workouts where you truly find results and success.

The grind and the discipline you get from being able to stick around when it's not glamorous, pretty, or fun is where success happens.

When your workouts feel boring, when you start feeling tired, that's when you're right at the edge of succeeding. That's not just true in the gym. That's true in business. That's true in every other important aspect of life. Training is a mirror for every other positive thing you will ever do.

Training Creates Energy

Spoon Theory is a philosophy of energy that is often used to describe chronic illness or disease. Basically, every "spoon" you have represents a certain unit of energy that you can use throughout your day.

If you want to take a shower, that's one spoon. If you want to walk the dog, that's another spoon. Going to the gym may be two spoons. You are given a specific amount of energy, then that's all you have for the day and therefore you need to plan accordingly.

Even without a chronic illness, many of us still have a limited amount of energy to use throughout the day. That is why at five, or six o'clock, we feel completely crushed, mentally fatigued, and slow to complete the daily requirements at our home or finish up at the office.

This is also why it can take us three hours to do an hour's worth of tasks in the second half of the day.

Training will give you more spoons. This does not apply to every workout or exercise, but if you take the training methodologies discussed here and progressively improve your conditioning in a structured way, that will give you the benefits of the physical and mental energy you want.

A stronger body and stronger discipline create a compound effect.

The Objective

Spend 20 minutes per day doing some sort of physical training.

There are so many ways to incorporate training into your life. I will give you two great options here, or you can go to n8trainingsystem.com/MDBMtraining to get the full Million Dollar Body Method 28-Day Program for gym or home.

If you are already training for 20+ minutes a few times per week, don't stop what you're doing. Keep that same program and add in 20 minutes of the cardio-based routines on the days when you're not doing your other program.

Physical training is the cornerstone for an unbreakable body and an unshakeable mind. Here's why:

- Training builds muscle faster than exercise. (Strength training in particular)
- Training builds self-esteem and confidence as you watch your daily improvements.

- Training builds the discipline and habits needed to be a juggernaut in your business and respected by your family.
- Training allows your body to better mitigate the effects of stress, making you happier and calmer.
- Strength training burns more fat long-term than cardio.
- Training builds energy in your body and allows you to be "on" when needed.
- Training releases endorphins and helps you have a positive attitude.
- Training builds focus by forcing you to be completely engaged in a singular task, much like meditation.
- Training makes you harder to kill, and more useful in general.

The Daily Investment

Train for 20 minutes daily.

Pick one or two abilities you want to work on, and alternate days. Or simplify and do the same thing every day but focus on getting a little better.

Note: Do not do 20 minutes of pushups every single day for 28 days. That will lead to overuse and injury quickly.

Cardio workout:

Bike, run, row, or swim for 10 minutes and see how far you get. Try to get a little faster when you do the second 10-minute interval. This can be as simple as running away from your house for 10 minutes, then running back.

Strength workout:

Pick a program you can do daily or go to n8trainingsy-stems.com/MDBMtraining to get access to the training program and nutrition I use to get incredible results with clients

Or go through this circuit as many times as you can in 20 minutes. Work on improving every day:

10 Pushups
15 V-ups
20 Squats
15 Rows
10 Reverse Lunges (*each side*)

Count how many rounds you get and work on improving over time.

Go to n8trainingsystems.com/MDBMworkout to see a video of this challenge if you are not sure how to do the above exercises.

Up Your Game

Doing the MDBM workout every day for 28 days will elicit a chance in how you look and feel, but the best possible option is having a program designed for you that can be done and tracked over the four weeks to the best possible effect.

There are many resistance-training programs out there, but most are not designed to be done in 20 minutes or less on a daily basis.

That is why I recommend you check out:

The MDBM Gym or Home Training Program

Simply head over to n8trainingsystem.com/MDBMtraining and sign up for the program. You will get workouts delivered in a way that's easy to read and execute and will never wonder what to do or how to do it.

I created this option after being asked on a regular basis what the ideal training recommendations would be. So, I created it for you.

Track your workouts

It should go without saying that in order to see progressive improvements day after day, the actual progress needs to be tracked. Luckily, there are many apps that can help you with this, or you can simply record everything in a note on your phone or a paper journal.

Split your weights and cardio

A simple way to improve your body composition and your cardiovascular capacity without worrying about overuse injuries is by doing resistance training one day and cardio the next.

Even if they are the same A and B workouts every week, you'll still see a marked improvement over the four weeks.

Switch the grip

If you are going to do the same program on a daily basis, switch up your grips, hand placements, and stances.

Pushups can become wide pushups, yoga pushups, diamond pushups, or pushups on handles.

Squats can become wide, narrow, or heel elevated.

Rows can be done wide, high (to your face), neutral, or underhand.

Get a TRX or suspension trainer

One of the best ways to get a complete training effect and be able to work all the muscles of your body even if you are training at home is to purchase a suspension trainer like a TRX.

This allows you to hit the muscles in the back and have access to hundreds more exercises than you can do with body weight alone

Training like this also has the added benefit of burning more body fat because of the nature of "closed-chain" exercises where you move your body through space.

Sample Schedule

Here's an easy way to fit these concepts in while maintaining the integrity of the Daily Investments.

These are suggestions and additions. As long as you're:

- Starting the day with 32 ounces of water and 60 seconds of explosive exercise
- Having a nutrient-dense protein shake for your first meal
- Having protein and veggies for lunch
- Having protein, veggies, and rice or potatoes for dinner
- Writing down your critical 3 for tomorrow
- Drinking one gallon of water per day
- Training 20 minutes per day

You'll be blown away by how much focus you have and how fast fat disappears.

6:00 a.m.: Wake up
6:10 a.m.: Drink 32 oz. water
6:25 a.m.: 60 seconds of explosive exercise
6:30-7:15 a.m.: Strength training

7:15-7:20 a.m.: Deep breathing and cooldown
7:20-7:30 a.m.: Cold shower and getting ready for the day
7:35 a.m.: Make and drink your protein shake
12:30 p.m.: Eat midday meal of protein and veggies
6:30 p.m.: Dinner of protein, veggies, and potato/rice
7:30 p.m.: Dessert of yogurt parfait
9:30 p.m.: Write down your critical three for tomorrow

WEEKLY INVESTMENT:

FAST 24+ HOURS EVERY WEEK

Many of us regard insurance as a scam or a bad thing that we "must" pay because we want to drive our cars.

But after getting into an accident, what does that relief feel like that you won't be liable to replace damaged parts, pay for a rental car, or shell out absurd amounts of money for medical bills?

One night, I was driving through Beacon Hill in Seattle to pick up some dinner with my wife and friend in the car.

We were driving down a steep hill that necessitated tapping the brake here and there to avoid picking up too much speed, when all the sudden

WHAM!

Out of nowhere, a car completely blew a stop sign and T-boned my car on the driver-side back panel.

We did a full 360-degree spin and wound up on the lawn of a house next to the street.

Like a bad dream, I got out of the car to make sure everyone is OK, and the other driver did the same.

Strangely, he asked me for my ID, which I did not give him. Another car stopped to see if we were OK, and while we were checking out the damage, someone said, "*Hey, did he just leave?*"

The driver from the other car had gotten back into his car and peeled out, leaving us standing there with our jaws on the ground.

Sure, people get in accidents. But not me.

Sure, hit and runs happen, but not to me.... right?

As I struggled to find any words to say that beyond "*WHAT AN ASSHOLE!*", my good friend Michelle wandered over to where his car was parked and bent down to pick up some trash off the ground.

Smiling, she turned around and held up his license plate that had come off in the accident! Justice would finally be served.

Unfortunately, that was not the case in the short-term. It ended up being a rental car from a tiny agency that refused to give up his information, but as it devolved into a long-term legal issue, we were still responsible for finding a new car as there was no payout in our immediate future.

Thankfully, our insurance stepped in and helped us with temporary transportation and making sure we did not suffer from an issue that could have otherwise been crippling.

Insurance is like a safety blanket.

It gives you the ability to keep your priorities in line even in the face of challenges and problems.

That's what fasting can do for us.

If we are eliminating 24+ hours of feeding from our week, our average weekly caloric intake drops by close to 15%. This can provide the nutritional insurance we need to continue to see fat loss even if other aspects of our nutrition fall off slightly.

That is why fasting is a must-have tool in your dietary toolbox.

There is a plethora of other benefits that come along with not eating for a full day, but the peace of mind and nutritional insurance is not to be underestimated.

Here's What I Know:

- Fasting improves insulin sensitivity and hunger signals
- Fasting provides nutritional "insurance"
- Fasting improves focus
- Fasting improves discipline

Fasting Improves Insulin Sensitivity and Hunger Signals

One study showed that the absolute fastest way to reset insulin sensitivity was done via fasting in as little as a two-week period. This means that in just two weeks, people were able to reset months or years of insulin resistance and become more sensitive to one of the chief hormones that is responsible for inflammation, belly fat gain, and low energy. [10]

As insulin sensitivity improves, we become more sensitive to our correct hunger signals. It becomes harder for us to mistake thirst for hunger signals, and we are hungry less often.

This also improves the sugar cravings that many of us have throughout the day, and keeps us from falling into patterns of snacking, which can sap our energy and promote belly fat gain.

Fasting also can highly improve cardiovascular disease markers as well as blood work. It's extremely easy to see that as you fast more, your blood work can improve, and you'll see results in your A1C levels, your fasting glucose levels, visceral fat levels, and inflammatory markers.

Fasting has also been shown to improve longevity as well as increasing telomere length. Telomeres are the "caps" on each strand of human DNA that protect our chromosomes.

Just like plastic tips at the end of shoelaces, they keep the strands from unwinding or unraveling. As we get older, those tips fray, and we experience the effects of aging faster.

Reducing food consumption on a regular basis, can keep us younger, longer.

Fasting also initiates autophagy, our body's natural detoxification mechanism. It is the time when our body can get rid of damaged cells, waste, and toxins, while rebuilding new cells. Only when we are not digesting can our body replace and rebuild tissue or other broken cells that need an upgrade.

The oldest living cell in our bodies is only seven years old. Some cells are replaced on a daily or weekly basis through this process. This makes it critical that we are taking in nutritious foods, because that is literally what is being used to rebuild our bodies.

Fasting Provides Nutritional "Insurance"

By simply including a 24-plus hour fast on a weekly basis, we are limiting or decreasing our average caloric consumption by up to one-seventh of what we would normally have.

This allows us to be a little bit more liberal in what we choose to consume in those other times. This DOESN'T mean that we need to go out and eat Cinnabon because we finished fasting for 12 hours, but it does give us more freedom to not be so structured and rigid at dinner, or not feel like we must limit ourselves from having foods we love.

This is one more reason why this style of eating can be critical to improving our ability to stick to the framework long-term.

Fasting Improves Focus

Currently in the world, there have never been more choices or distractions available to us.

Whether our phone, social media, or the food we are eating, we're always at war with something that demands our attention. Fasting is an amazing way to eliminate the distractions that come from eating and making choices surrounding food.

When we are doing deep work or are in flow state, something as simple as going back and answering an email that takes us a minute can detract an additional 15- 30 minutes from us because of how long it takes to get back to the flow state we were in beforehand.

Fasting is an amazing way to improve upon our willpower and our focus by eliminating many of the distractions that come along with food and beverages.

Fasting improves neural autophagy and increases our number of brain cells. Neural autophagy is how your brain cells recycle the waste material and repair themselves. Brain health is dependent upon this process and interfering with it can increase our brain's degeneration rate. Without proper autophagy processes because of lack of sleep or constantly digesting food, our brains deteriorate at a rapid rate.

Fasting also improves memory by increasing the brain's levels of brain-derived neurotrophic factor (BDNF). This is a protein that our brains create that regulates memory, learning, and higher cognitive function. Low levels of BDNF are linked to Alzheimer's, poor cognitive function, and poor memory.

Taking a break from eating also helps you take a step back from food addiction, something that is a uniquely human experience. An alcoholic might never have a drink again, but someone with a poor relationship with food still must eat regularly.

We are constantly bombarded and presented with myriad choices of what we should be eating at any given moment. Not only should we be snacking, but the food we eat SHOULD be delicious, exotic and cause our brain chemicals to go wild. Or at least that is what commercials tell us.

Fasting deliberately pulls us out of that mindset and allows our focus to sit somewhere else. We have now made a binary decision where we won't be tempted or engaged in looking for something to eat or drink because we know our next meal comes at a specific time and a specific place.

It is also amazing to see how much time we spend thinking about food after removing those temptations from our lives for even a short period of time.

> "If you want to get more done in life, eat less food." - Robin Sharma

Fasting Improves Discipline

Training even when you do not feel like it is done in the pursuit of benefits you might not be able to see or feel yet.

Fasting is the same. It enables us to train our brains to delay gratification for something better than a sweet snack. When we can delay physical and emotional pleasure on a regular basis in pursuit of higher goals, we become an unstoppable force of determination and grit.

It is staggering how many high-functioning, incredibly intelligent adults struggle with eliminating snacking, or eating poorly.

Most of the time it comes down to the fact that they have not made A DECISION.

Fasting eliminates the need to waiver or vacillate on what you are eating, because you've already decided you will not be eating until a certain time has elapsed.

This idea of making it extremely binary, no longer *"I might,"* but rather, *"I will,"* creates freedom. You are not stuck pondering if this is the 1% of the time when you should snack or have a treat. It's simply "not now."

And in no case is that more true than discipline with our nutrition and our diet.

> "Discipline equals freedom."
> -Jocko Willink

The Objective

Fast 24 hours weekly.

A 24-hour fast is a ritual that requires planning and sacrifice. It forces you to say, "I'm not eating right now," and to fill that time by doing other things that you may not have time for on a daily basis.

If you ever fast on a weekend, it's eye-opening because it shows you how much time we spend thinking about and planning our food daily.

NOTE: *Doing a 16 hour fast with an 8-hour feeding window is popular with several diets right now. It is not something you need to do as a part of the Million Dollar Body Method, but if you like that style of eating, you can easily adapt it to this framework simply by pushing your first meal back to 11 or 12. Your lunch would go around 3 or 4, and then dinner would be at its normal time.*

If you are using a 16/8 hour fasting schedule, you will still do the 24 hour fast weekly, but do not push the time any longer than 24 hours.

Fasting every week is a game-changing nutritional habit. Here's why:

- Fasting gives you close to a 15% reduction in weekly calories, perfect for fat loss or providing "nutritional insurance."

- Fasting can eliminate faulty hunger signals caused by insulin resistance.
- Fasting can increase insulin sensitivity to normal levels after just two weeks.
- Fasting during the day can provide more focus and energy to help you be more efficient in your work.
- Fasting improves discipline and helps us make nutrition binary.
- Fasting turns on "autophagy," our body's natural detox mechanism.
- Fasting improves mental clarity.
- Fasting improves brain function.
- Fasting is correlated with longevity and decreased risk of Alzheimer's.
- Fasting decreases likelihood of stroke or diabetes.
- Fasting makes you more badass because of a decreased reliance on the emotional crutch of food.
- Weekly fasts train your body to burn stored fat for fuel.

The Daily Investment

Fast for 24+ hours every week.

For most of us, it's sufficient to start your fast after an early dinner on Tuesday, then eat a later dinner on Wednesday. This is a great place to start your personal fasting protocol.

Wednesday is just a suggestion; I'd advise doing it on any day that you're busy.

Up Your Game

There are many varieties and lengths of fasts you can include. Here are some simple ways to get more out of your fast:

Fast every day

A 16-hour fast daily can be ideal for men. However, a 12-hour window without eating is a great practice for everyone. That might mean no after-dinner snacks, which is the best choice for most of us.

Fast longer

Studies show that 24-72-hour fasts can have positive effects. After the three-day mark is when our bodies can start eating into muscle tissue and affecting sleep. This isn't worth it unless there's a result beyond the physical that you're pursuing.

Pushing the fast longer can have additional benefits, as well as imparting important information about our bodies and minds.

1. **Easy:** Fast from an early dinner one day until a later dinner the next day. 24 hours.
2. **Level up:** Fast from dinner one day until breakfast 2 days later. i.e., eat Tuesday night and then eat again Thursday morning.
3. **Challenge mode:** Fast 48+ hours from dinner one day until dinner (or longer) 2 days later.

I'd highly suggest doing a 72-hour fast at some point outside of this program (training sessions get tough on day three). It's an eye-opening experience about your relationship with food and focus.

Drink plenty

During a fast, it's important to get enough water to help the autophagy process as well as facilitating fat loss and keeping energy high.

However, it's also acceptable to have black coffee or tea during the fast. You'll be amazed at what one cup of coffee will do for you on day two of your fast.

If going longer than 24 hours and still training, you can include Branched Chain or Essential Amino Acids (BCAAs or EAAs) after training to maintain and rebuild muscles.

This causes a brief spike in insulin, but it only lasts 2-3 minutes as digestion isn't needed to absorb calorie-free liquids.

Plan your first meal

Make sure you know what you're going to eat for the meal that breaks the fast. It's easy to get into a "bender" mindset and crush all kinds of food if you have not planned correctly and stop your fast in the food court at a mall.

The best thing to break your fast with is veggies, specifically leafy greens, or carrots. This can give you a shot of nutrient-dense foods that will be absorbed exceptionally well after a 24-hour fast.

Sample Schedule

Here's an easy way to fit these concepts in while maintaining the integrity of the Daily Investments.

These are suggestions and additions. As long as you're:

- Starting the day with 32 ounces of water and 60 seconds of explosive exercise
- Having a nutrient-dense protein shake for your first meal
- Having protein and veggies for lunch
- Having protein, veggies, and rice or potatoes for dinner
- Writing down your critical 3 for tomorrow

- Drinking one gallon of water per day
- Training 20 minutes per day
- Fasting 24 hours once per week

You'll be blown away by how much focus you have and how fast fat disappears.

6:00 a.m.: Wake up
6:10 a.m.: Drink 32 oz. water
6:25 a.m.: 60 seconds of explosive exercise
6:30-7:15 a.m.: Strength training
7:15-7:20 a.m.: Deep breathing and cooldown
7:20-7:30 a.m.: Cold shower and getting ready for the day
7:35 a.m.: Make and drink your protein shake
12:30 p.m.: Eat midday meal of protein and veggies
6:30 p.m.: Dinner of protein, veggies, and potato/rice
7:00 p.m.: Stop eating for 24 hours
9:30 p.m.: Write down your critical three for tomorrow

THE MILLION DOLLAR BODY METHOD

The 28-Day Program

As we've gone through each piece in depth, my goal was to show you specifically what you need to do in order to:

1. Create FOCUS for your finances and family time.
2. Burn FAT for your physique and health

All without losing valuable time on marathon workouts or lengthy meal prep.

I hope that you have seen how this framework is backed by science to create the best result possible in the shortest amount of time for those two specific goals.

And while I do not think this is the very best diet for building muscle or preparing for a marathon, this IS the very best diet in the world for engineering superhuman focus, which can lead to fat loss and muscle gain week by week, for as long as you continue to use the tools outlined in this book.

And that's the big difference.

When people tell me they love keto or lost X amount of weight on a carnivore diet, I always ask, "*How long have you been doing it?*"

For some, it has been days or weeks. Some people make it into the months, but rare is the time that I hear someone say they've been following a protocol for a year or longer.

When I ask my clients and others who have followed this framework from the beginning, they simply say, "*This is how I eat now.*" The lifestyle change will always win over the flash in the pan, even if the other option comes in a big red box with a lot of great marketing behind it.

In the next chapter, I'm going to break down the mentality most of us will progress through during the course of the 28 days so you can avoid common pitfalls.

After that, I will describe easy ways to continue using this framework while adding in the foods you love to make it completely your own.

That's the other great thing: You are not locked into one style of eating for the rest of your life. You don't have to abstain from desserts or drinks, but you now have the tools you need to fit the foods you love into your life in a way that makes sense for your Focus, Family, and Physique.

I know people that use Glycogen Priming with a paleo diet, Atkins, and Mediterranean. So, it's possible as an adaptation of the current way you eat. You can make it work no matter what foods you love because it starts with energy.

The Full Program

Every day for the next 28, we're going to hit our 7 Daily Investments. Those are:

1. High ROI Morning Routine - Drink 32 ounces of water and do 60 seconds of explosive exercise within 30 minutes of waking up.
2. The Entrepreneur's Breakfast - Make a protein shake for your first meal of the day.
3. The Start-Up Lunch - Eat only protein and veggies for lunch.
4. The CEO Dinner - Eat a dinner of meat, veggies, and either rice or potatoes.
5. Final Deposit - Write down your critical three tasks for tomorrow before bed.
6. Liquid Assets - Drink one gallon of water per day.
7. Work Hard, Train Harder - Train for 20 minutes daily.

Our weekly investment is: *Fast for 24+ hours*

Go to n8trainingsystems.com/MDBMcalendar to get a free copy of the MDBM 28-day calendar so you can check the boxes off as you go.

100% compliance on these 7 Daily Investments will change your life.

- You're going to lose fat.
- You're going to sleep better.
- You're going to change your relationship with food.
- You're going to improve your blood markers.

You're going to be able to do all these things without lengthy meal prep times or extended times in the gym.

This revolutionary nutrition framework can change your life.

But there's one thing you MUST have if you want the benefits described above.

Belief.

You bought this book, and you have read this far, so you're clearly looking to make a change.

But if you come to this program with skepticism, or seeking out problems, you are going to find them.

If you come in with the belief that we have already done the heavy lifting, the testing, the tweaking, and the research to make sure that we're bringing you a concept that can totally change your life, you're going to find results.

This is the main reason that I see why people fail.

If two people start this program at the same time but one goes all in with BELIEF, while the other is skeptical and looks for holes and pitfalls, the first person will get great results and learn new skills that can change their life. And the second person will end up with YET ANOTHER nutrition or fitness plan that "didn't work" for them.

Which are you?

What attitude are you bringing to the next 28 days?

THE MILLION DOLLAR BODY METHOD WEEKLY MINDSET

We've all tried new things before.

Diets, fitness programs, new hobbies. Some of them have gone well, but there are always some that we look back on and say, "What were we thinking?"

To avoid falling into common pitfalls, I want to walk you through the mentality that comes with The Million Dollar Body Method.

Here's generally what happens during the first few weeks:

Week 1: Excited

When we're starting something new that promises to deliver a big result that we've been looking for, we're excited.

Maybe you got coerced into this, but hopefully you're amped up about the next phase of your fat loss and focus journey.

The big goal in Week 1 is to ONLY follow the program even though it might seem "too simple." That's the majority of the feedback I get from most hard-charging Type-A entrepreneurs.

They wonder when the HIIT workouts, the marathon workouts, the chicken and broccoli, the 90-min morning routines, and the sweat lodge sessions are going to take place.

Answer? Never.

This program is designed to deliver a high ROI without you needing to get a nanny or hire a new employee. You should be able to fit this into a complicated and busy lifestyle without missing a step, and that's the beauty of it.

When you do get busy, when things fall apart, you can always come back to your baseline of this program to drop fat and regain insane focus.

It's always going to be here for you without requiring ultimate sacrifice to see results.

The focus for Week One is **SIMPLICITY**.

Don't overdo it, don't add anything else in, and approach the program like a scientist. As you change some of your inputs, take note of how you feel and what the scale says.

Make sure to record your weight and take a picture of yourself if the physical results are important to you.

Week 2: Dialed In

After your first week of changing your inputs, adding a 24-hour fast in, and getting 20 minutes of training every day, you WILL see some cool results.

Most people experience a sharp uptick in energy and focus during the day, decreased sugar cravings, better sleep at night, and a few lbs. of fat loss.

There are two general responses to this. One is going harder, doing more, and trying to get even better results.

This is the right way to approach this, just make sure you are improving by adding in more from the "Up Your Game" sections, rather than haphazardly adding in additional training, cleanses, or anything that's not in the Million Dollar Body Method.

The other option that many people subconsciously fall into is getting laxer because the results were "too good to be true" in the first week. So if they try a little less, fast for a few less hours, have a few more carbs with breakfast, they'll still get half the results.... right?

Do not fall into this trap.

There's a time and a place to get more lax and find easier options, but that doesn't happen in Week 2. We will discuss how to fit this into a regular lifestyle outside of the structured MDB Method in the next chapter. But for the first 28 days, we need to have our eyes on the prize and take the time to let our body get the results we're looking for.

The focus for Week 2 is **CONSISTENCY**.

You don't HAVE to do more, but make sure you're not doing less, either.

Week 3: Intensity

In Week 3, we are approaching the time frame it takes to build a habit. Your breakfast should feel easy to make, and your lunch should be simple to plan.

You are probably getting into a rhythm with grocery shopping and planning your meals as well.

Week 3 is magic, don't forget that.

Week 3 is when many people see the biggest results of the program, but it also coincides with some of the meals and prep starting to seem boring or rote.

At Week 3, we should also be feeling a marked difference in our insulin resistance and sugar cravings. This is the week when we would expect to see the blood markers improving and our bodies becoming more adept at partitioning the right nutrients and feeding muscle cells instead of fat.

Now is the time we want to improve and start striving for perfection in the training, the morning routine, and the meals.

The focus for Week 3 is **INTENSITY**.

Start seeing what you're capable of in your training. Push yourself a little harder. Extend the fast a bit longer.

Like getting a vintage car tuned up and rebuilding the engine, now is a good chance to see what you're capable of.

See how it feels to dive deep into a task that requires high concentration and focus and stay on it for longer than you normally would.

Test yourself in your workouts. Run a little bit longer and a little bit harder. Fast for 48 hours instead of 24.

Choose something hard and see how you do.

Week 4: Recommit

Week 4 is normally when people start looking for alternatives to some of their meals.

We've found meals and training that get us results we enjoy, but also other things that we don't love quite as much.

It's only natural that we start experimenting a little with our meals and branching out with our tastes. Especially as the program ends, it's easy to shift back to "normal" eating.

We are not normal.

At this point, remind yourself why you picked up this book and started the program in the first place. Was it to look great naked? Gain superhuman focus? Make more money? Have a simple framework for nutrition that does not interfere with your cash flow?

Whatever it is, remember what it feels like to pursue and achieve those goals.

The focus for Week 4 is **COMMITMENT**.

Recommit to the goals you set and the framework to get you there.

This is not a "diet" in the traditional sense that creates restriction, lethargy, and regression.

This is a framework for how you can eat moving forward that will keep you focused and looking your best.

So, what are you going to commit to moving forward?

Upon completing this program, many people will maintain it six days per week and then have one day per week that they don't worry about the specifics. If you're a "pancakes on the weekend" type of person, that could be a good fit.

Just make sure you know WHY you started in the first place, and commit yourself to the important goals you set.

The goals are the destination. The Million Dollar Body Method is the path.

WHAT'S NEXT? HOW TO HAVE YOUR CAKE AND EAT IT, TOO

Now that you've had four weeks to dial in your framework, it's time to broaden your food choices to include things that you enjoy and try new combinations.

Rice and potatoes are excellent carb sources, but a life without pasta or tortillas is a good way to feel deprived of the foods you love.

Since you're at the point where you've gotten back to being insulin sensitive, you've reset your sleep, and you can instantly create extraordinary focus on demand, you'll be more aware when foods no longer agree with you or serve your goals.

So if you come off of the MDBM and have a big bowl of pasta with alfredo sauce and sleep terribly, that is a good clue that something in that meal doesn't serve you.

Similarly, if you find that other meals give you headaches, cause bloating, gas, decreased focus or poor sleep, write them down so you can figure out which of the ingredients no longer match your goals. Maybe it's the pasta, maybe it's the sauce, maybe it's the 30 gummy bears you ate after dinner. Hard to say.

The easiest way to continue to follow this framework is by continuing to eat similar to how you did throughout the program but adding new meals to your repertoire as you find ones that fit the framework as well as the feels you're looking for.

So, don't go changing everything at once. That's not scientific and defeats one of the best things that came out of the 28-day program. Your ability to *feel* the effects that food has on us.

Most of us don't notice a difference because we never give ourselves a break from sugar and processed food to feel what it's like to be insulin sensitive and functioning at our maximum output.

Don't blow that by changing everything on Day 29.

The Framework

This is the nutrition formula for superhuman focus and rapid fat loss. This is the baseline. This is where you can always come back to when you need to improve your results or your output.

BREAKFAST	LUNCH	DINNER
• Protein • Fat	• Protein • Veggies	• Protein • Carbohydrate • Veggies

The Options

Here are the best possible options for each of the macronutrients, proteins, carbohydrates, and fats.

Plug and play these within the framework to try out different meals and combinations that you and your family will enjoy.

Make sure to use salt, pepper, and other seasonings as you experiment. There's nothing worse than a bland, roasted veggie that could have been delicious with a minimal amount of oil, salt, and pepper.

Some foods are combinations as well. Steak is a protein and a fat, and quinoa is a protein and a carb. For the sake of simplicity and to avoid overcomplication, I have added each one to the column with the macronutrient that they have the *most* of.

If you want a more in-depth look at these macronutrient breakdowns, this is covered in depth in the Million Dollar Body Community on Facebook. Go to n8trainingsystems.com/group to get free access.

These are listed in order from "most ideal" to "least ideal", but most can be substituted in when creating your meals after the 28 day program concludes.

So yes, you can eat a dinner of shellfish, carrots, and cereal and still be in alignment with the program. But we don't want cereal, bread, or pasta as our carbohydrate every night.

I also don't list any veggies here. All vegetables are awesome for you. Eat them with abandon.

CARBOHYDRATES	PROTEIN	FAT
• Rice	• Chicken Breast	• Avocado
• Sweet Potato	• Turkey Breast	• Coconut milk
• Potato	• Bison	• Nuts
• Oats	• White Fish	• Avocado Oil
• Beans	• Shrimp	• Coconut Oil
• Fruit	• Tuna	• Olive Oil
• Pasta	• Protein Powder	• Egg Yolk
• Bread	• 90%+ Lean Beef	• Peanut Butter
• Cereal	• Egg White	• Butter
	• Shellfish	• Bacon

Of course, this does not tell the full story of all the foods that are combinations of the main macronutrients.

Like most things in life, the answers are rarely black and white, so here are the foods that combine protein and either fats or carbs that can be integrated in your nutrition plan moving forward.

This will require some testing with your personal preferences and food selections, I just wanted to give you options to plug and play into the framework that we developed over the course of this program.

PROTEIN/CARBOHYDRATE COMBINATIONS	PROTEIN/FAT COMBINATIONS
• Quinoa • Legume + Grain (i.e., black beans and white rice in combination) • 2% Milk • Plain Greek Yogurt • Cottage Cheese • Tofu • Soybeans	• Steak • Salmon • Lamb • Whole Eggs • Whole Milk • Full Fat Dairy • Cheese • Sausage

The final combination is one that we should avoid when looking for superhuman focus and rapid fat loss. These foods should be generally avoided, especially when we need to have a productive and high energy day.

When you look at this list, it will be obvious that none of the foods listed are great for our waistline or focus.

CARBOHYDRATE/FAT COMBINATION
• Enchiladas
• Pizza
• Sweetened Yogurt
• Crackers
• Burgers
• Potato Chips
• Creamy Dressings
• Muffins
• Cake
• Ice Cream
• French Fries

The Training

The next steps with your training are simple, but not easy.

To achieve the highest level of focus and fat loss daily, we need to incorporate some kind of movement habit every day. This can be as simple as going for a walk or attending a yoga class.

Consistency is the key to everything you're looking for.

But in order to truly have and maintain a Million Dollar Body, we need to incorporate resistance training 2-3 days per week.

Whether this is done in a gym or at home using a suspension trainer is up to you and your time constraints, but at the very minimum, this is something that needs to be a priority for as long as you want to have a lean, muscular, energetic body.

If you use the specific training protocols from the Million Dollar Body program (n8trainingsystem.com/MDBMtraining) you can continue to use those and expand upon them after the 28-day program.

Find a coach or a training protocol that can give you the workouts you need based on the specific goals you are pursuing in the moment as well. If writing training protocols isn't your full-time job, hire someone to help you train for your event or the body you want. You'll shortcut your success and stay injury free while you do it.

FREQUENTLY ASKED QUESTIONS

What about snacking? I didn't see any of that on the program.

As discussed at length, we want to get away from snacking as much as possible.

Snacking is the enemy of both fat loss and focus. Here's why:

- Snacking causes digestion which activates "rest and digest" mode.
- Snacking triggers hunger signals later in the day.
- Snacking doesn't allow us to pull from stored fat and reinforces that our bodies should burn the food we eat first.
- Snacking does not allow us to become more sensitive to hunger vs thirst signals.
- Snacking does not allow us to become more insulin sensitive.
- The more often we eat or snack, the less energy we have and the faster we age.

So, unless you're working your ass off doing something you shouldn't need to snack. If you feel like you do, always ask yourself:

- Am I hungry or just thirsty?
- Do I need this food or am I eating out of habit or boredom?

Do I have to have protein with every meal?

We should be striving to have protein at every meal. Not just on this program, but for the rest of our lives.

Protein is satiating, critical for health and building a lean body, and EXTREMELY difficult for your body to convert to fat.

This makes it one of the best things to eat in order to maintain a lean body because we don't need to eat as much. We can also rest assured that when we are eating, it's serving our goals of a lean muscular body as well as ensuring that we can have superhuman focus without feeling bogged down from a rich meal.

What about the Million Dollar Body Method for vegetarians?

It's extremely tough to get enough protein on a vegetarian or vegan diet without having a ton of carbs during the day.

So, it really depends on the style of vegetarian you are. If you are OK with having Whey Protein (derived from dairy), you could easily have a protein shake in the morning, eggs and veggies at lunch, then a large, nutritious meal at dinner.

For example, combining legumes (beans) with grains can give you a complete amino acid profile, like what you would get from eating animal products, but since you're combining two carb sources, the carb load would be much higher.

This would be totally fine at dinner, but it would not be ideal for breakfast or lunch.

If you're fully vegan or don't want to consume any animal products whatsoever, the Million Dollar Body Method isn't your best choice.

What about dessert and eating after dinner?

We can easily incorporate some sort of dessert or snack after dinner with this style of eating.

Simply go a little lighter on your carbs for dinner to give yourself a little bit of wiggle room here. That's all you *need* to do to make sure you're good to go! That's the beauty of this program.

Although with that in mind, I still would not recommend having cake, pie, or ice cream nightly. That counteracts a bit of the insulin sensitivity we're looking for.

You CAN however have the Greek yogurt, protein, and berries, or cottage cheese and fruit nightly.

Another favorite that I will incorporate from time to time, especially with clients that are looking to add more muscle size, is after-dinner cereal.

Simply add a scoop of collagen to your milk or almond milk and then whisk it up (or put it in a shaker cup and shake it up). Add your cereal on top and you've got a muscle-building carb and protein treat.

How can I do this with 16/8 Intermittent Fasting?

Glycogen priming is simple with a 16-hour fast and an 8-hour feeding window. Simply continue to eat light during the day and have your biggest meal at night.

For most people, this means shifting the protein shake or breakfast meal to midday, having a small protein and veggie snack in the afternoon, then a bigger dinner at night.

I've also seen some of the busiest people in the world have success with just two meals per day: the protein and fat shake for their first meal, and then a bigger dinner.

Try both and see which one fits your schedule and lifestyle the best.

Can I drink alcohol?

Any amount of alcohol beyond zero is suboptimal for fat loss and focus.

But I know that things come up, we get invited to holiday parties, our clients order a bottle of wine, or sometimes you end up at the airport at 8a.m. To think that no one would have any alcohol on this program is asinine.

So, here's how to do it in the smartest way possible.

1. Stick to clear liquors, and no sugary mixers.
2. Don't drink and eat within an hour of each other
3. Have one glass of water for every glass of booze you imbibe.
4. Before you drink, have a meal higher in proteins and fats, and lower in carbohydrates.

But how do I know how much I'm eating?

One of the brilliant things about this framework is that we can get great results in our focus and fat loss without having to monitor and weigh every calorie.

By letting our body adapt and be able to send us clear signals, it becomes clear when we've overeaten or need additional food.

Of course, if you're curious how much you're eating, or in what ratios, you may want to consider tracking your food for a period of time in order to figure out your numbers.

What if I'm not losing weight?

Since we don't advocate for tracking as a part of this method, there can be a tendency to overeat certain things.

Fats have 9 calories per gram, and carbohydrates and proteins have only 4 calories per gram.

So, if you're "eyeballing" your peanut or almond butter in the morning and giving generous pours of oil onto all your foods, you might not see the fat loss you want.

If that's you, take these two steps.

1. Start by measuring out your portions, especially the fats. Make sure you're getting a single serving of each. This can often fix any plateaus.
2. Log and measure your foods for a time. This will require weighing out certain dishes, but it will also give you a deeper knowledge of the foods you're eating and help you know when you've gone over your daily caloric allotment.

This happens mostly in sedentary populations that aren't getting a lot of movement on a daily basis, OR when first starting an exercise routine that is primarily cardio-based.

Cardio can increase hunger, so you might burn 300 calories during the workout, but be starving afterward and eat an additional 500.

If that's the case, don't stress! Just track your food, and we can dial in over time.

References

1. National Highway Traffic Safety Administration. Research on Drowsy Driving. http://www.nhtsa.gov/Driving+Safety/Drowsy+Driving. Accessed August 18, 2020.
2. Younossi, Zobair M. "Nonalcoholic Fatty Liver Disease and Nonalcoholic Steatohepatitis: Implications for Liver Transplantation." Liver Transplantation, vol. 24, no. 2, 2018, pp. 166–170., doi:10.1002/lt.25003.
3. Harvie, M N, et al. "The Effects of Intermittent or Continuous Energy Restriction on Weight Loss and Metabolic Disease Risk Markers: a Randomized Trial in Young Overweight Women." International Journal of Obesity, vol. 35, no. 5, 2010, pp. 714–727., doi:10.1038/ijo.2010.171.
4. Sanburn, Josh. "One More Reason to Hit the Gym: You'll Make More Money at Work." Time, Time, 8 June 2012, business.time.com/2012/06/08/one-more-reason-to-hit-the-gym-youll-make-more-money/.
5. "Caffeine: How Much Is Too Much?" Mayo Clinic, Mayo Foundation for Medical Education and Research, 6 Mar. 2020, www.mayoclinic.org/healthy-lifestyle/nutrition-and-healthy-eating/in-depth/caffeine/art-20045678.

6. Foo, Yong Zhi, et al. "The Carotenoid Beta-Carotene Enhances Facial Color, Attractiveness and Perceived Health, but Not Actual Health, in Humans." Behavioral Ecology, vol. 28, no. 2, 2017, pp. 570–578., doi:10.1093/beheco/arw188.
7. Afaghi, Ahmad, et al. "High-Glycemic-Index Carbohydrate Meals Shorten Sleep Onset." The American Journal of Clinical Nutrition, vol. 85, no. 2, 2007, pp. 426–430., doi:10.1093/ajcn/85.2.426.
8. Tang, Y.-Y., et al. "Short-Term Meditation Induces White Matter Changes in the Anterior Cingulate." Proceedings of the National Academy of Sciences, vol. 107, no. 35, 2010, pp. 15649–15652., doi:10.1073/pnas.1011043107.
9. Thornton, Simon N. "Increased Hydration Can Be Associated with Weight Loss." Frontiers in Nutrition, vol. 3, 2016, doi:10.3389/fnut.2016.00018.
10. Anton, Stephen D., et al. "Flipping the Metabolic Switch: Understanding and Applying the Health Benefits of Fasting." Obesity, vol. 26, no. 2, 2017, pp. 254–268., doi:10.1002/oby.22065.
11. "Perceived Insufficient Rest or Sleep Among Adults-- United States, 2008." PsycEXTRA Dataset, 2009, doi:10.1037/e552162010-003.